Easy Nine-Patch Quilting™

Edited by
Sandra L. Hatch and Jeanne Stauffer

HOUSE of
WHITE
BIRCHES
PUBLISHERS
SINCE 1947

Easy Nine-Patch Quilting

Editors: Sandra L. Hatch, Jeanne Stauffer

Associate Editor: Barb Sprunger

Copy Editor: Cathy Reef

Photography: Tammy Christian, Nora Elsesser, Teri Staub

Photography Assistants: Linda Quinlan, Arlou Witwer

Production Manager: Vicki Macy

Creative Coordinator: Shaun Venish

Production Artist: Brenda Gallmeyer

Traffic Coordinator: Sandra Beres

Technical Artist: Connie Rand

Production Assistants: Shirley Blalock, Carol Dailey, Cheryl Lynch

Book Design: Dan Kraner

Publishers: Carl H. Muselman, Arthur K. Muselman

Chief Executive Officer: John Robinson

Marketing Director: Scott Moss

Editorial Director: Vivian Rothe

Production Director: Scott Smith

Printed in the United States of America

First Printing: 1998

Library of Congress Number: 97-76987

ISBN: 1-882138-32-5

Every effort has been made to ensure the accuracy and completeness of the instructions in this book. However, we cannot be responsible for human error, for the results when using materials other than those specified in the instructions or for variations in individual work.

Versatile Nine-Patch

One of the most simple patterns to create is the Nine-Patch. Even though the primary version is made with nine equal squares, the possibilities for design are endless. Throw in divisions in each square or unequal Nine-Patch designs and you can see how easy it is to change a simple design to a more complicated one.

Whether you are a geometry whiz or not, designing patterns from a square that has been equally divided in nine parts is easy. Using a ruler, each section of the Nine-Patch may be divided again and again, changing the overall design—the basic design still remains a Nine-Patch. Curves and arcs may be drawn in the squares to make even more complicated designs. Add fabric designs and different values to the block equation and you have discovered the fun part of designing.

Although patterns and instructions in this book all include specifics for the quilts shown, you can create your own versions of the designs by changing fabric colors and the placement of lights and darks. Enjoy playing with design, color and value on paper to create even more designs based on the ideas from our designers.

Today we are blessed with the best of tools and equipment that make the construction of quilts quicker and easier. We share the design process with our quilting foremothers, but we have so many advantages when it comes to the process of construction.

As you browse through this book, remember that you have many choices when you decide which projects to make for yourself. As you plan your version of the project, your vision may vary from ours. Remember that some designs are formed by the placement of lights and darks, so choose fabrics with similar values if you want to keep the pattern formation the same as the quilt shown, but be creative and have fun.

CONTENTS

Easy Nine-Patch Quilting

Glorious Nine-Patch Quilts

Contemporary Nine-Patch

General Instructions

Nine-Patch Through the Years

By Xenia Cord

One of the simplest pieced designs used in quiltmaking is the Nine-Patch. The design lends itself to numerous variations, permuting into complexities that bear little resemblance to the original block.

Among the popular pattern-source references available today, one lists 124 patterns based on the Nine-Patch; another illustrates more than 600 designs based on nine equal units, or designs that are related but are based on nine unequal segments. The patterns range from simple concepts such as the Nine-Patch block itself to Variable Star to Maple Leaf to varieties of Feathered Star as shown in Figure 1.

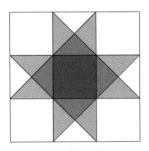

Variable Star

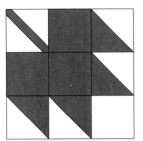

Maple Leaf

Feathered Star

Figure 1
These designs are all based
on the Nine-Patch.

Before the invention of the sewing machine, hand sewing was the basis for the construction of all garments, household linens, quilts, curtains—indeed, it is difficult to think of a single textile item in common use in the home on which some hand-sewing was not required. Skill with a needle defined femininity, so it is little wonder that girls began sewing instruction at a very early age. In America's 18th century and into the early 19th century, girls attended special schools where hand sewing was one of the most important skills

taught. Sewing lessons worked into samplers of needle skills including stitching verses such as the following:

Of female arts in usefulness
The needle far exceeds the rest,
In ornament there's no device
Affords adorning half so nice.

Mastery of this skill at home was often initiated by setting the child to cutting and then sewing together small squares of fabric. Interest could be added by varying the colors and the size of the squares. As the sets of sewed squares multiplied, the child might see how the construction of a quilt top could be accomplished.

Nineteenth-century reminiscences and published secondary sources refer frequently to the early age at which girls were instructed in hand sewing and in quiltmaking; beginning to sew straight seams at the age of 3 or 4 was not unknown. In the days before the sentimentalization of childhood, children were expected to be functioning members of the family at an early age, and were expected to be profitably busy. Idle hands being the devil's workshop was a commonly held belief.

The devastating effects of the Civil War made new life all the more precious, and children in the second half of the 19th century enjoyed a more leisurely childhood. Girls, however, were still expected to be proficient at needlework, and remnants of this tradition extended into the present century.

The task of hand-sewing blocks was not always accomplished without problems. A woman who grew up to become editor of a popular quilt magazine recounted her experience: "I have three sisters, and my mother taught us all how to sew when we were about 3. She still tells the story of how my sister sewed her appliqué to the background fabric and her dress when she was only 4 years old."

Another woman was forced to make Nine-Patch blocks at the age of 5. She accidentally sewed one of the block seams to her skirt, and rather than destroy the laboriously sewn seam, she cut a hole in her skirt to free the handwork. She so disliked the task of making blocks that she never completed the quilt top, leaving it to be finished 75 years later by her niece.

As with all pieced quilt designs, there are several ways in which the Nine-Patch design can be varied. These include manipulation of the design itself by halving or quartering or even further dividing each of the nine components; by changing the way the blocks are set together; by varying the use of color; by choosing special fabrics which themselves provide a design element; and by using the blocks as a vehicle for another important concept, such as signatures. The quilts discussed in this chapter and shown here and elsewhere in the book employ all of these variations; three are antique works from the same decade of the 19th century and two are recent.

Continuous Nine-Patch

Basic Nine-Patch blocks can be set straight and separated by sashing, they can appear on point with sashing or alternate plain squares, and they can be set block-to-block, without separation. The *Continuous Nine-Patch* shown here consists of hundreds of 3" blocks, each hand-pieced with 1" squares. The blocks are then set together without sashing to create the overall impression of a red-and-blue quilt. But the quiltmaker has actually made blocks in several sets of colors, and has then arranged them so that when the quilt is viewed in its entirety, diagonal bands of colors appear. We can visualize the quiltmaker laying her carefully made blocks out on a floor to check for pattern continuation and color harmony. Then perhaps she picked up

each row of blocks in order, stringing a knotted thread through them to keep them stacked until she could sew them together.

Because this *Continuous Nine-Patch* was made in the 1880s when bright turkey-red prints and vivid indigo-blue prints were popular, the quiltmaker had a wide variety of fabrics from which to choose. Perhaps she traded or begged different prints from her friends or purchased remnants from some textile mill. We can also see, looking closely at the prints, that she included a number of odd conversation prints among her choices.

In the last quarter of the 19th century, conversation prints containing tiny images and whimsical scenes became an important part of the textile market. Certainly dating from the American Centenary, and continuing through the 1890s, object prints were produced for the retail market in quantity and in hundreds of designs.

Common themes were equestrian, celestial and nautical designs, oriental motifs and sports items capitalizing on the new game of baseball, the growing popularity of bicycle riding and other outdoor activities for all ages. While these fabric designs were apparently produced for the home-sewing and apparel market, they are most usually seen as little pictures featured in small units of pieced quilts.

Nine-Patch on Point

The American Centennial also gave rise to a number of commemorative fabrics featuring patriotic images. The

Nine-Patch on Point shown on the previous page features a fabric celebrating the Marquis de Lafayette as a part of its block components, complete with a laurel wreath around his head. Lafayette was only 20 years old when he arrived from France to be commissioned as a major general in George Washington's Continental Army, and his participation and accomplishments were romanticized in the years following the Revolution. This popular hero's triumphant tours of the new country in 1784 and 1824 even spawned a pieced quilt pattern, Lafayette Orange Peels. Along with other Centennial images in cloth, Lafayette appears in quilts from the decades after 1876. Using specialty fabrics like these in any quilt gives it an extra dimension.

effect of halving the fours of the Nine-Patch block into diagonal segments creates an entirely different design. The fact that the back and front of this quilt are entirely in strong, dark colors makes the centers of the blocks even more effective, and points to the importance of the inscriptions. The quilt is from Bucks County, Pa., but little else is known of these inscribers and their purpose for coming together on the quilt. However, the quilt must have been considered special by its custodian, because it has survived to the present without ever having been washed.

Like the previous quilt, *Cut Glass Dish* is based on Nine-Patch, but with multiple sub sets of half-square triangles. Only the center, upper right and lower left units of the basic block are left undivided. The pattern is meant to resemble the facets of cut or pressed glass, and is most interesting when executed in multiple or scrap colors. This particular quilt is a contemporary one, but made entirely of vintage fabrics from the 1920s through the 1940s, and has no matching prints. As such, it is a variation of a charm quilt, which traditionally has only one pattern piece and no repeating fabrics. Additionally, this quilt shows a great

Variable Star/Ohio Star

Cut Glass Dish

Occasionally quilts have been used as a focus for another purpose beyond the purely functional. When individuals drew together in kinship or friendship to honor a special individual or event, or to raise funds for an issue or place, quilts were often used as the vehicle through which the activity was conducted. A customary feature of such quilts was the inscribing of names in central sections of the design. In the example shown here, the Variable Star/Ohio Star block based on Nine-Patch was executed in double pink and bold 1880s prints, two fabrics per block, with a center square in starkly contrasting white, on which a name is inscribed. The simple many conversation prints of the period, including several early Disney fabrics. It caused the maker no end of fun and organization in finding and then keeping track of the more than 860 fabrics used. By making the square, two ends were accomplished: The even rows of blocks allowed the creation of peach-and-white pinwheels in a large-scale echo of the Nine-Patch concept, and the quilt will fit a king-size bed.

This is only one example of how the basic units of Nine-Patch can be divided to create a new design. If the corner and center segments are divided into smaller Nine-Patch units and the larger blocks joined alternately with squares of background fabric, Single Irish Chain is the result; if those sub sets are Four-Patches and the remaining units are divided into two triangles as shown in Figure 2, the pattern is The Railroad/Jacob's

Ladder/Road to California. Card Trick, Corn & Beans, Double T—all are based on Nine-Patch; the varieties seem endless. And some of the most interesting creations appear when blocks form a secondary pattern as manipulation of colors and fabrics highlights certain segments.

Milky Way

Milky Way, shown here in crib size, is one such example. The basic Nine-Patch has sub sets of Four-Patches in the corners, with a solid center. Using the background fabric with the center color to make half-squares in the remaining segments creates a center pinwheel. The positive/negative effect of the background fabric creates a second star or pinwheel when the blocks are joined.

Nine-Patch is a versatile design that has delighted quiltmakers for nearly two centuries of American quiltmaking. It lends itself readily to beginner efforts and fascinates more advanced quilters with the effects of sophisticated multi-part design. Clearly it remains a traditional favorite that provides endless variety.

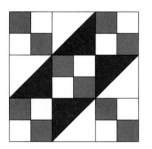

The Railroad

Jacob's Ladder

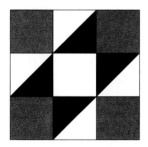

Road to California

Card Trick

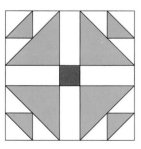

Corn & Beans

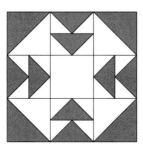

Double T

Figure 2
More designs based on the Nine-Patch.

Grandmother's Nine-Patch Favorites

Before rotary cutting and strip piecing were heard of, Grandmother made Nine-Patch quilts. She cut up tiny squares left over from sewing clothing or other household items or she cut them from worn-out clothing. She might have used her machine to stitch the squares together, but there were not many shortcuts.

You can make quilts like Grandmother's using much quicker methods and still get the look of an antique using reproduction prints available in shops today. Make a connection with the quilters from the past while making a quilt for the future.

Continuous Nine-Patch

By Xenia Cord

Made in the Bay City, Mich., area in the 1880s, this Nine-Patch quilt uses many 1" conversation print squares. If you have lots of scraps, this *Continuous Nine-Patch* is your next project. Work on it a little at a time until blocks are complete. Without the diagonal arrangement of same-color blocks, one would not be able to distinguish one Nine-Patch block from another.

Instructions

Step 1. Cut 1 1/2" by fabric width strips from a wide variety of light and dark fabrics to total 66 strips each value, or a total of 132 strips.

Step 2. Sew a dark strip to a light strip to a dark strip; repeat, using about half of the strips. Sew the remaining half of the strips in a light/dark/light configuration. Cut all strips into 1 1/2" segments.

Step 3. Arrange three segments to make a variety of primarily light and primarily dark blocks as shown in Figure 1. Repeat for 422 blocks.

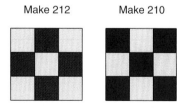

Make 212   Make 210

Figure 1
Make a variety of primarily light and primarily dark blocks as shown.

Step 4. Cut 20 maroon print strips 1 1/2" by fabric width; set aside 10 strips. Cut eight blue print strips 1 1/2" by fabric width.

Step 5. Sew a maroon strip to a blue strip to a maroon strip; repeat for four strip sections. Cut each strip set into 1 1/2" segments. Sew a blue strip to a maroon strip to a blue strip; repeat for two strip sets. Cut each strip set into 1 1/2" segments.

Step 6. Arrange the maroon/blue segments in rows to

Project Specifications

Skill Level: Intermediate
Quilt Size: 66" x 78"
Block Size: 3" x 3"
Number of Blocks: 528

Materials

✔ 6 yards total light and dark scraps
✔ 1 yard maroon print
✔ 1/2 yard blue print
✔ 1/2 yard navy print
✔ 1/4 yard brown print
✔ Backing 70" x 82"
✔ Batting 70" x 82"
✔ Neutral color all-purpose
✔ Quilting thread
✔ Basic sewing supplies and tools

make one Nine-Patch block as shown in Figure 2; repeat for 54 blocks.

Step 7. Cut eight navy print strips 1 1/2" by fabric width. Using the remaining maroon print strips, sew a maroon strip to a navy strip to a maroon strip; repeat for four strip sets. Cut into 1 1/2" segments. Sew a navy strip to a maroon strip to a navy strip; repeat for two strip sets. Cut strip sets into 1 1/2" segments.

Make 54   Make 52

Figure 2   **Figure 3**
Make maroon and   Make maroon and navy
blue blocks as shown.   blocks as shown.

Step 8. Arrange the maroon/navy segments in rows to make one Nine-Patch block as shown in Figure 3; repeat for 52 blocks.

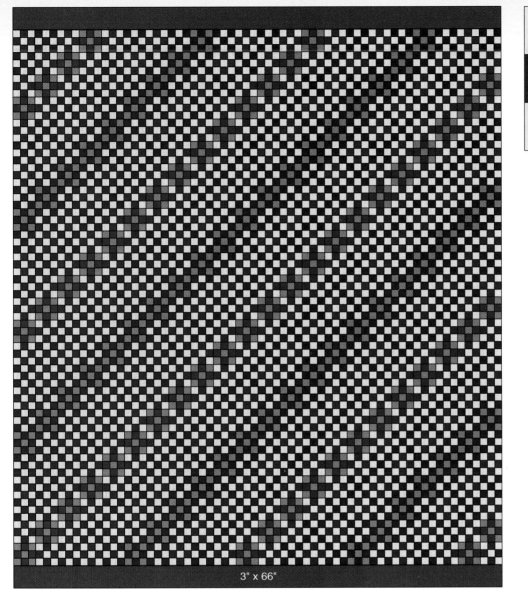

Nine-Patch
3" x 3" Block

Continuous Nine-Patch
Placement Diagram
66" x 78"

Step 9. Arrange the pieced blocks in 24 rows of 22 blocks each, placing the maroon/blue blocks and the maroon/navy blocks to create a diagonal pattern referring to the Placement Diagram. Join the blocks in rows; join the rows to complete the pieced center. ***Note:*** *It is important to number rows as they are stitched. With 24 rows to work with and a diagonal pattern to maintain, it would be easy to mix up rows and create lots of ripping-out time.*

Step 10. Cut two strips brown print 3 1/2" x 66 1/2". ***Note:*** *Strips will need to be pieced to make correct*

length. Sew a strip to the top and bottom to complete pieced quilt.

Step 11. Prepare top for quilting and finish referring to General Instructions. ***Note:*** *This top has no open areas for a fancy quilting design, and quilting in the ditch of every seam would take a lifetime. Quilting in the ditch of each block and perhaps on both diagonals would be an option. Tying the layers at block intersections is another good option. The quilt shown was quilted on the diagonal in every other block.*

Rainbow of Rings

By Carol Scherer

Making the Nine-Patch blocks for this quilt is the easy part! Putting them together is a bit more complicated. The original maker found that out when she put her quilt together, as you can see from the interruption of the rings on the quilt.

Project Notes

The quilt shown was made in the 1930s using pastel prints from that era. Our instructions do not recommend putting the blocks together in the exact same manner as the quilt shown. Although many of the rows are consistent as to the placement of the A hexagon, some are not. When the placement of A is changed, the pattern does not make the allover concentric circles. Notice that the circles are not always the same size on the quilt.

If you look at the drawings given in Figure 7, where lines have been removed, the pattern does make the same-size circles throughout.

You may prefer the mixed-up look, but if you want the pattern to really show, be very careful when sewing the blocks together to get all A pieces with points going up and down.

Instructions

Step 1. Prepare templates using pattern pieces given. Cut as directed on each piece. *Note: Strips of muslin and prints may be cut 1 1/2" wide, stitched together and cut in 1 1/2" segments as shown in Figure 1. If a planned color arrangement is used, this is recommended.*

1 1/2"

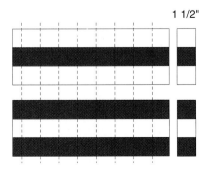

Figure 1
Join strips in 2 sets; cut each set in 1 1/2" segments.

Project Specifications

Skill Level: Experienced
Quilt Size: Approximately 70" x 90"
Block Size: 3" x 3"
Number of Blocks: 318

Materials

- 2 1/2 yards total of various light and dark prints
- 5 3/4 yards muslin
- Backing 74" x 94"
- Batting 74" x 94"
- Off-white all-purpose thread
- 1 spool off-white quilting thread
- Basic sewing supplies and tools

Step 2. Sew a muslin B to a scrap B to muslin B to make a row; repeat. Sew a scrap B to a muslin B to a scrap B to make a row.

Step 3. Join the pieced B rows as shown in Figure 2 to complete one Nine-Patch Block; repeat for 318 blocks.

Figure 2
Join strip sets to make 1 Nine-Patch block.

Step 4. Join a Nine-Patch block to each side of A; set in C pieces to complete one block as shown in Figure 3; press. Repeat for 53 blocks.

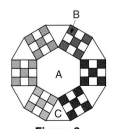

Figure 3
Sew a Nine-Patch block to each side of A;
set in C to complete 1 block.

Step 5. Join eight blocks in a row with C pieces as shown in Figure 4; repeat for four rows. ***Note:*** *When piecing, be careful to place piece A with points going from top to bottom rather than side to side. Piece D may be substituted for piece C to eliminate some seams. Doing this complicates row construction and makes piecing units necessary. It is really easier to use piece C with more seams than to substitute D. We have given piece D for those who prefer this method, but we give no drawings or instructions for using this piece except for the drawing given in Figure 6.*

Step 6. Join seven blocks in a row with C pieces as in Step 5; repeat for three rows.

Step 7. Join the rows, setting in C as necessary as shown in Figure 5.

Step 8. Mark the quilting design given in piece A.

Step 9. Prepare top for quilting and finish referring to General Instructions**.**

Figure 4
Join 8 blocks with C
pieces for 1 row.

Figure 5
Join block rows with
C pieces as shown.

Figure 6
Piece D may be substituted for piece C to
eliminate seams. ***Note:*** *This complicates
piecing as complete blocks may not be
stitched and then joined in rows in the same
construction manner given here.*

Figure 7
Change the position of A and notice how
design changes.

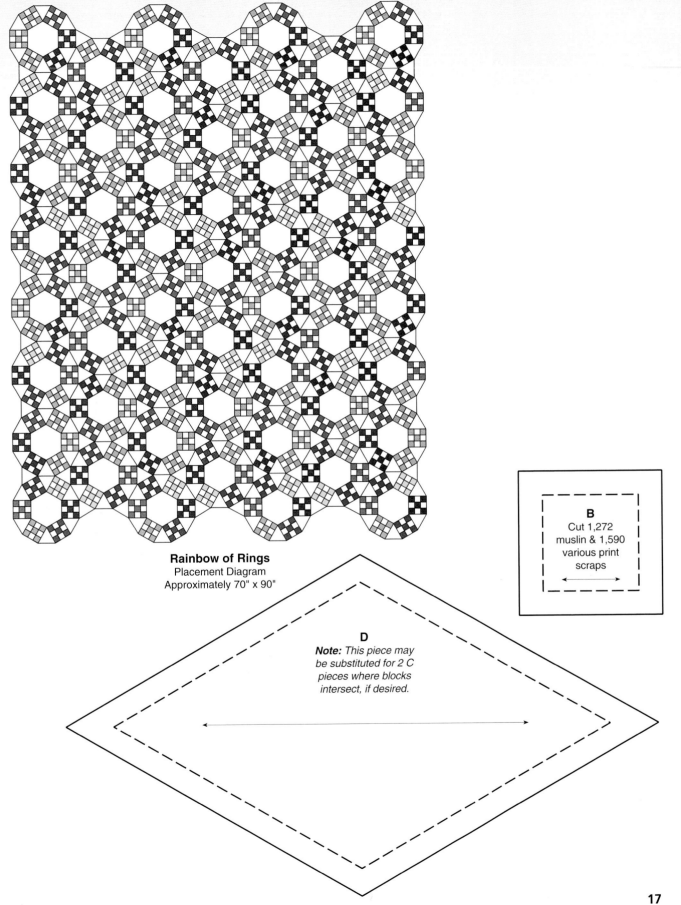

Rainbow of Rings
Placement Diagram
Approximately 70" x 90"

B
Cut 1,272
muslin & 1,590
various print
scraps

D
Note: *This piece may
be substituted for 2 C
pieces where blocks
intersect, if desired.*

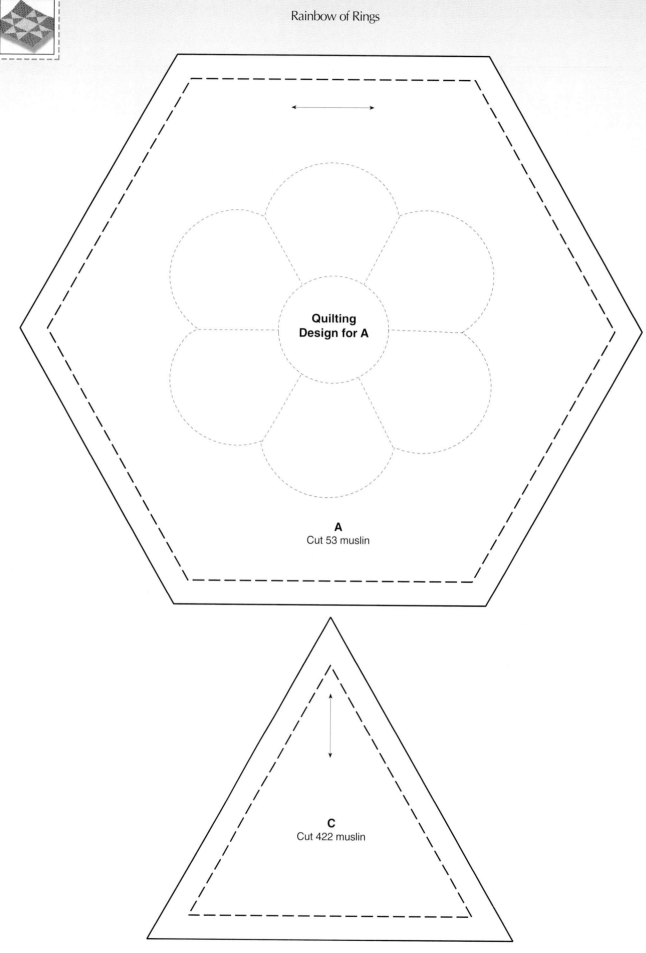

**Quilting
Design for A**

A
Cut 53 muslin

C
Cut 422 muslin

Musical Chairs

By Sandra L. Hatch

This simple Nine-Patch design was not found in any of the pattern identification books. I called it Musical Chairs because it looks like the triangles are crowding around each square. There may be an official name somewhere, but I like this one.

Project Notes

The project shown began as a partially pieced top. Some rows were missing blocks and other rows were inaccurately pieced. To make a useful item out of what I had, I removed some sections and repaired others. I did leave some of the original top alone; therefore, the seams don't all meet accurately.

As I finished this top, I wondered about its history. Who made it? Did one person piece the blocks and another person try to put them together? If so, why was it left with partially finished rows and leftover blocks? Why were the blocks hand-pieced when the top was put together by machine?

Of course there are no answers. The top was in a box my mother gave me. She bought it at a yard sale and did not really know any history about it. Although it is not really colorful, it is a neat collection of shirting prints and other fabrics from another era. It fits into almost any color scheme and makes a great table covering.

I decided to combine both hand and machine quilting to continue the methods used by the maker or makers.

Instructions

Step 1. Prepare templates using pattern pieces given. Cut as directed on each piece to complete one block. Repeat for 18 blocks. *Note: Quick cutting and piecing methods may be used, but when using scraps for blocks it is not recommended. If using a planned color arrangement, use templates to determine strip sizes, referring to General Instructions for methods.*

Step 2. To piece one block, sew four B triangles to C; repeat for four B-C units. *Note: In the sample shown, some C squares are dark and some are light. When C is light, B is dark. Notice that all blocks do not have the same contrast as scraps were used. If you prefer the*

Project Specifications

Skill Level: Intermediate
Quilt Size: 50" x 50"
Block Size: 7 1/2" x 7 1/2"
Number of Blocks: 18

Materials

- ✔ A variety of light and dark scraps for blocks
- ✔ 1 yard gray/black print for unpieced squares
- ✔ Backing 54" x 54"
- ✔ Batting 54" x 54"
- ✔ Gray all-purpose thread
- ✔ 1 spool off-white quilting thread
- ✔ Basic sewing supplies and tools

scrap look, remember to select fabrics to help make the design stand out as shown in Figure 1. Figure 2 shows how insufficient contrast can change the block.

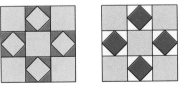

Figure 1
The drawings show how the design stands out when darks and lights are placed properly.

Figure 2
When there is little contrast, the design does not show as well.

Step 3. Arrange the B-C units with A squares to make rows as shown in Figure 3. Join blocks in rows; press. Join rows to complete one block; press. Repeat for 18 blocks.

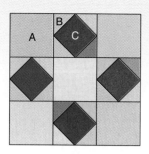

Musical Chairs
7 1/2" x 7 1/2" Block

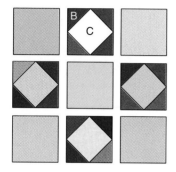

Figure 3
Arrange A squares with B-C units in rows.

Musical Chairs
Placement Diagram
50" x 50"

Step 4. Cut 18 squares black/gray print 8" x 8".

Step 5. Arrange pieced blocks with squares in rows as shown in Figure 4. Join blocks in rows; press. Join rows; press.

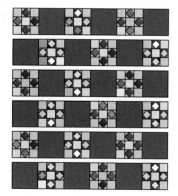

Figure 4
Arrange pieced blocks with black/gray squares in rows.

B
Cut 16 light
or dark

A
Cut 5 light or dark
Cut 76 scraps for borders

C
Cut 4 light or dark

Step 6. Cut 76 squares from a variety of lights and darks. Piece 18 squares together for one side border; repeat. Sew to opposite sides; press. Piece 20 squares together twice for top and bottom borders. Sew to top and bottom; press.

Step 7. Mark your favorite quilting design in the black/gray print squares.

Step 8. Prepare top for quilting and finish referring to General Instructions.

20

Cut Glass Dish

By Xenia Cord

It isn't easy to identify some Nine-Patch blocks. The Cut Glass Dish is one of those blocks. The Nine-Patch sections are further divided into Four-Patch sections. This quilt is a challenge to make because of color arrangement, but the results are well worth the effort.

Project Notes

There are 864 different conversation prints from the 1920s to the 1940s used in the quilt shown. Quick cutting and piecing methods are difficult to use when every piece is different. If strips cannot be cut, cut squares the size instructed to cut strip segments and continue instructions, piecing 864 triangle/square units and completing quilt as directed.

The centers of five blocks have a pinwheel design instead of plain squares, and the pinwheels turn in different directions.

Instructions

Step 1. Cut 31 strips white solid 2 7/8" by fabric width; repeat with scrap strips.

Step 2. Cut all strips into 2 7/8" segments; cut segments in half on the diagonal to make triangles. Sew a white triangle to a scrap triangle on the diagonal to make a triangle/square as shown in Figure 1. Press seams toward scrap triangle; repeat for 864 triangle/squares.

Figure 1
Sew a white triangle to a
scrap triangle to make a
triangle/square.

Step 3. Join four triangle/squares to make a square unit as shown in Figure 2; press. Repeat for 216 units; set aside.

Project Specifications

Skill Level: Intermediate
Quilt Size: 96" x 96"
Block Size: 24" x 24"
Number of Blocks: 9

Materials

- ✔ 6 yards white solid
- ✔ 2 1/4 yards peach print
- ✔ 1 yard peach solid
- ✔ 3 1/2 yards total scraps for triangles
- ✔ Backing 100" x 100"
- ✔ Batting 100" x 100"
- ✔ Neutral color all-purpose thread
- ✔ 1 spool white quilting thread
- ✔ Basic sewing supplies and tools

Figure 2
Join 4 triangle/square units to
make a square unit.

Step 4. Cut two strips each white solid and peach solid 4 7/8" by fabric width. Layer a white strip with a peach strip right sides together, aligning edges perfectly. Cut layered strips into 4 7/8" segments; repeat for 10 segments.

Step 5. Cut segments on the diagonal to make triangles. Sew together along diagonal edge to make triangle/squares for Pinwheel design; press. Repeat for 20 peach/white triangle/squares; set aside.

Step 6. Cut six strips white solid 4 1/2" by fabric width. Cut strips into 4 1/2" segments; repeat for 52 segments.

Step 7. Cut four strips peach solid 4 1/2" by fabric width. Cut strips into 4 1/2" segments; repeat for 36 segments.

Step 8. Arrange pieced and cut segments in rows referring to Figure 3 to complete one block with Pinwheel center. *Note: Three blocks have pinwheels turning in one direction while two blocks have pinwheels turning in the opposite direction. Refer to the Placement Diagram for arrangement.* Stitch units together in rows; join rows to complete one block; press. Repeat for five Pinwheel-center blocks. Referring to Figure 4, complete four square-center blocks.

Step 9. Arrange blocks in three rows of three blocks each referring to the Placement Diagram for positioning of blocks and placement of Pinwheel design. Join the blocks in rows; join rows to complete pieced center; press.

Step 10. Cut eight each white solid and peach solid squares 2 3/8" x 2 3/8". Cut each square in half on one diagonal to make triangles. Sew a white triangle to a peach triangle to make a triangle/square unit; repeat for 16 units. Join four units as shown in Figure 5 to make a small Pinwheel square for border corners; repeat for four blocks.

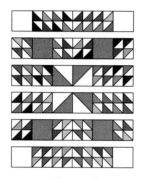

Figure 3
Complete block in rows with a
Pinwheel block in the center.

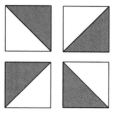

Figure 5
Join 4 units to make a small
Pinwheel block.

Step 11. Cut four strips peach print 3 1/2" x 72 1/2". Sew a strip to the top and bottom of the pieced center; press seams toward strips. Sew a small Pinwheel square to each end of the remaining two strips. Sew to opposite long sides; press seams toward strips.

Step 12. Cut two strips white solid 9 1/2" x 78 1/2". Sew to opposite sides of pieced center; press seams toward strips. Cut two more strips 9 1/2" x 96 1/2"; sew to top and bottom. Press seams toward strips; round corners if desired.

Step 13. Prepare top for quilting and finish referring to General Instructions.

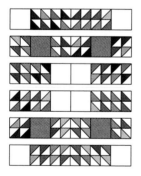

Figure 4
Complete block in rows using plain
squares in center.

Cut Glass Dish
24" x 24" Block
Pinwheel Center

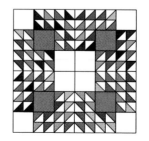

Cut Glass Dish
24" x 24" Block
Plain Center

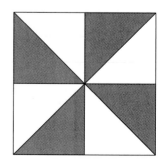

Pinwheel
3" x 3"

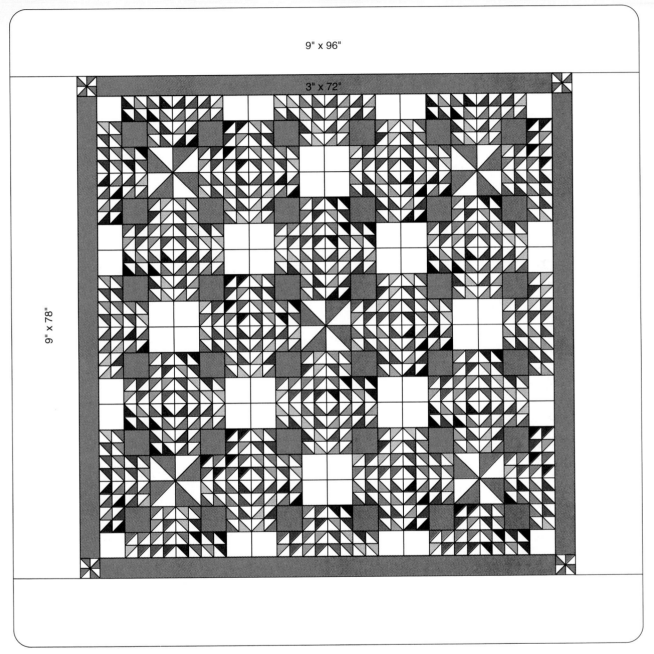

9" x 96"

3" x 72"

9" x 78"

Cut Glass Dish
Placement Diagram
96" x 96"

Antique Nine-Patch

By Pauline Lehman

The Nine-Patch block is set on point in this antique scrap quilt. Each block uses only one print with muslin, and some fabrics are used to make several blocks. Here is the perfect opportunity to use up scraps from your collection.

Project Notes

It is difficult to give quick cutting and piecing instructions because scrap fabrics are used. If you prefer to use these methods, cut muslin strips in 2 1/2" x 14" lengths and combine with scrap strips of the same length referring to the General Instructions or other projects for methods when using strips.

Instructions

Step 1. Cut 14 strips muslin 2 1/2" by fabric width. Cut strips into 2 1/2" segments.

Step 2. Cut five 2 1/2" x 2 1/2" squares medium or dark scraps for each block. You will need 56 blocks. *Note: More than one block from each scrap color may be used or each block could be different. The quilt shown has several colors repeated, some more than four times.*

Step 3. To piece one block, sew a scrap square to a muslin square to a scrap square to make one row; repeat. Sew a muslin square to a scrap square to a muslin square to make another row.

Step 4. Join the rows as shown in Figure 1 to complete one block; press. Repeat for 56 blocks.

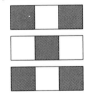

Figure 1
Join rows to
complete 1 block.

Step 5. Cut 42 squares muslin 6 1/2" x 6 1/2".

Step 6. Cut seven squares muslin 9 3/4" x 9 3/4". Cut each square across both diagonals as shown in Figure 2 to make side fill-in triangles.

Project Specifications

Skill Level: Beginner
Quilt Size: 75 1/2" x 84"
Block Size: 6" x 6"
Number of Pieced Blocks: 56

Materials

- 5 3/4 yards bleached muslin
- 1 1/2 yards total medium to dark scraps (a 2 1/2" x 14" strip is needed for each block)
- Backing 79" x 88"
- Batting 79" x 88"
- Off-white all-purpose thread
- 1 spool off-white quilting thread
- 9 yards self-made or purchased binding
- Basic sewing supplies and tools

Step 7. Cut two squares muslin 5 1/8" x 5 1/8". Cut each square once on the diagonal to make corner triangles.

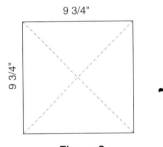

Figure 2
Cut 9 3/4" squares on both diagonals to
make side fill-in triangles.

Step 8. Arrange triangles with pieced blocks and solid squares in diagonal rows as shown in Figure 3. Join the units in rows; press. Join the rows; press to complete pieced center.

Step 9. Cut two strips muslin 8 1/2" x 60". Sew to top and bottom of pieced center; press seams toward strips. Cut two more strips 8 1/2" x 84 1/2". Sew to opposite long sides; press seams toward strips.

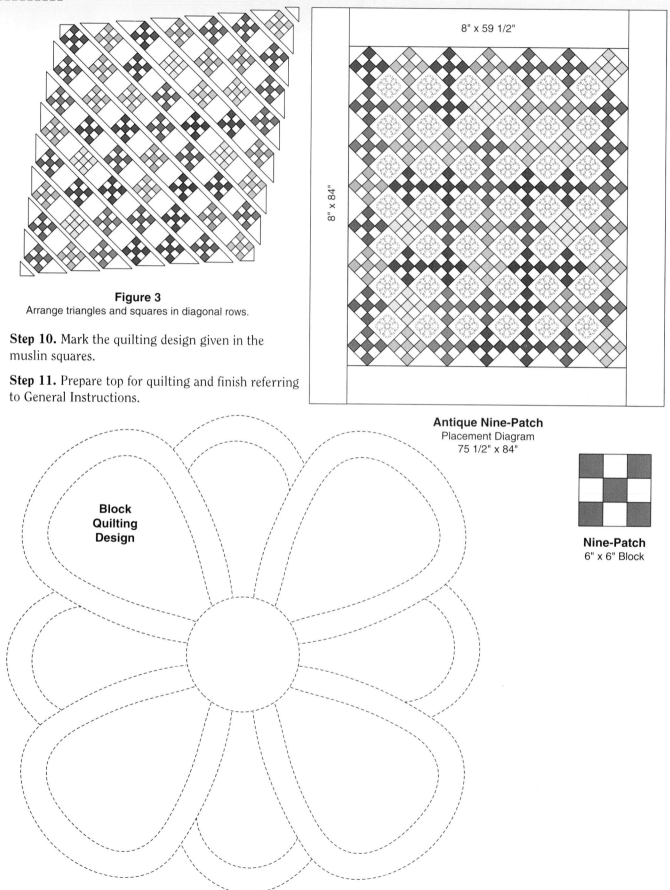

Figure 3
Arrange triangles and squares in diagonal rows.

Step 10. Mark the quilting design given in the muslin squares.

Step 11. Prepare top for quilting and finish referring to General Instructions.

8" x 59 1/2"

8" x 84"

Antique Nine-Patch
Placement Diagram
75 1/2" x 84"

Block Quilting Design

Nine-Patch
6" x 6" Block

Eight-Pointed Star

By Sandra L. Hatch

The Eight-Pointed Star design is one of the most popular and basic Nine-Patch patterns. There are countless variations from simple to complex. This antique scrap version has an unusual setting. Each block combines only two fabrics, a light and a dark value. The blocks are set together with wide sashing strips on the diagonal without borders. If you like the antique look, antique reproduction fabrics may be found at your local quilt shop.

Instructions

Step 1. Cut one square light print and four squares dark print 3 1/2" x 3 1/2".

Step 2. Cut two squares each light and dark prints 4 1/4" x 4 1/4". Cut each of these squares on both diagonals to make triangles as shown in Figure 1.

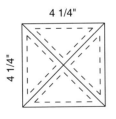

Figure 1
Cut squares on both
diagonals as shown.

Step 3. Sew a light triangle to a dark triangle on the short sides as shown in Figure 2; repeat for all triangles.

Figure 2
Sew a light triangle to
a dark triangle on
short sides.

Project Specifications

Skill Level: Intermediate
Quilt Size: 63 3/4" x 80 3/4"
Block Size: 9" x 9"
Number of Blocks: 31

Materials

- 31 pieces each light and dark prints 9" x 12" or 1 1/4 yards each light and dark prints
- 3/4 yard pink-on-pink print
- 2 yards green print
- Backing 68" x 85"
- Batting 68" x 85"
- 8 3/4 yards self-made or purchased binding
- Coordinating all-purpose thread
- Basic sewing supplies and tools

Step 4. Join two triangle units to make a square as shown in Figure 3; repeat for four squares.

Figure 3
Join 2 triangle units
to make a square.

Step 5. Arrange the pieced squares with the 3 1/2" x 3 1/2" squares to make a block as shown in Figure 4. Join the pieces in rows; press. Join the rows to complete the block; press. Repeat for 31 blocks.

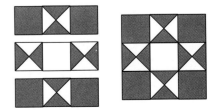

Figure 4
Arrange pieces to make a block.

Eight-Pointed Star
Placement Diagram
63 3/4" x 80 3/4"

Step 6. Cut 32 sashing squares pink-on-pink print 3 1/2" x 3 1/2".

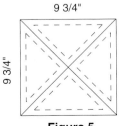

Figure 5
Cut squares on both diagonals.

9 3/4"

9 3/4"

Step 7. Cut 80 sashing strips from green print 3 1/2" x 9 1/2".

Step 8. Cut five squares 9 3/4" x 9 3/4" pink-on-pink print. Cut each square on both diagonals to make four triangles as shown in Figure 5.

Step 9. Arrange the pieced blocks, sashing strips and squares and pink triangles in diagonal rows as shown in Figure 6. ***Note:** At this time all sashing strips are still rectangles with no angled cuts. The angles will be trimmed later.*

90-degree angle using any square as a guide for cutting as shown in Figure 8 to complete top.

Figure 7
Trim sashing strips even
with edge of triangles.

Figure 8
Trim corner sashing at
a 90-degree angle.

Figure 6
Arrange blocks, squares, strips and triangles in diagonal rows.

Step 10. Join the units in diagonal rows; press. Trim sashing strips even with edges of outside-edge triangles as shown in Figure 7. Trim corner sashing strips at a

Step 11. Prepare top for quilting and finish referring to General Instructions.

Floral Bouquet

By Chris Carlson

intage '30s fabrics combine to make the tiny Nine-Patch blocks that appear as flowers in this pretty miniature quilt. Use quick methods to create accurate pieces to make construction easy.

Instructions

Note: A 1/4" seam allowance is included in all measurements. Spray all limp or wrinkled fabric with fabric sizing first and iron for more accurate cutting and easier piecing. Cut block log strips and border and binding strips on the lengthwise grain of the fabric.

Cutting

Step 1. Stack the six assorted 5" x 5" floral print squares. Cut the following from each: one 1" x 3" piece for A and two 1" x 1" pieces for A1.

Step 2. From the dark pink solid cut the following: six 1" x 1" pieces for B; four 2 1/2" x 2 1/2" squares for O; two 1" x 9" R binding strips; and two 1" x 13 1/4" P binding strips.

Step 3. From the light pink solid cut the following: 12 pieces 1" x 3" for C; six 1" x 2" pieces for D; six 1" x 2 1/2" pieces for E; one 11" x 22" piece (with 11" measurement on the lengthwise grain) for F; and one 6" x 11" piece for G.

Step 4. From the dark green solid cut the following: one 11" x 22" piece (with 11" measurement on the lengthwise grain) for H; and one 6" x 11" piece for I.

Step 5. From the medium blue solid cut the following: two 5 1/2" x 5 1/2" squares for J; two 3 1/2" x 3 1/2" squares for K; two 3" x 3" squares for L; four pieces 1" x 2 1/2" for Q binding strips; and four 1" x 3 1/2" pieces for S binding strips.

Step 6. From the blue-and-pink floral print cut the following: two strips 2 1/2" x 13 1/4" for M; and two strips 2 1/2" x 9" for N.

Piecing Blocks

Note: Sew with about 14–16 stitches per inch when sewing strips. Sew with about 12–14 stitches per inch

Project Specifications

Skill Level: Beginner
Quilt Size: 13" x 17 1/4"
Block Size: 3" x 3"
Number of Blocks: 9

Materials

✔ 1 piece each 5" x 5" of 6 assorted small floral prints
✔ 11" x 18" piece dark pink solid
✔ 22" x 24" light pink solid
✔ 1 fat quarter each dark green and medium blue solids
✔ 12" x 15" piece blue-and-pink floral print
✔ Backing 16" x 20"
✔ Lightweight batting 16" x 20"
✔ Fine machine thread
✔ Spray sizing for fabric
✔ Basic sewing supplies and tools, 3" x 18" ruler, BiRangle 4" x 7 1/2" ruler by Mary Hickey, Baby Bias Square 4" ruler by Nancy J. Martin, No. 60 or 70 machine needle

for remainder of piecing. If using BiRangle and 3" x 18" rulers, reverse cutting directions if you are left-handed. Press seam allowances in the direction of the small arrows or as directed. Avoid pressing bias edges; steam pressing is recommended.

Step 1. Sew a C piece to opposite sides of A to make one C-A-C strip set; press seams open and trim off 1/16". Cut two 1"-wide segments from the strip for rows 1 and 3 referring to Figure 1.

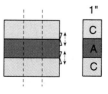

Figure 1
Sew C to A to C; cut 2 segments 1"
wide from strip for rows 1 and 3.

Step 2. Sew an A1 square to a B square to an A1 square to make one A1-B-A1 strip; press seams open and trim off 1/16". Cut two 1"-wide segments from the strip for row 2 referring to Figure 2.

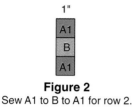

Figure 2
Sew A1 to B to A1 for row 2.

Step 3. Join rows 1, 2 and 3, matching seams, to complete one Nine-Patch block as shown in Figure 3. Repeat with remaining five fabrics to make six Nine-Patch blocks.

Figure 3
Join rows 1, 2 and 3 to
make a Nine-Patch block.

Step 4. Press and square up blocks to 2" x 2" if necessary.

Step 5. Sew one D strip to the right side of one block to make one unit as shown in Figure 4; repeat for six units. Press seams toward strips.

Figure 4
Sew D to a Nine-Patch block.

Step 6. Sew an E strip to the top edge of one unit to make one block as shown in Figure 5; repeat for six blocks.

Figure 5
Sew E to top.

Step 7. Press blocks on both sides; square up to 2 1/2" x 2 1/2".

Step 8. Layer F and H pieces wrong side up. Fold in half from the left, matching the 11" edges on the right as shown in Figure 6.

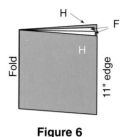

Figure 6
Fold pieces as shown.

Step 9. Place the BiRangle ruler on the upper edges of the fabrics. Place the 3" x 18" ruler on the diagonal line of the BiRangle ruler so that the lower right corner of the long ruler intersects the lower right corners of the fabrics to create a diagonal line across the fabric as shown in Figure 7. Remove the BiRangle. ***Note:*** *If you do not have the rulers listed, make templates for F, FR, H and HR using full-size pattern drawing given.*

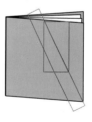

Figure 7
Lay rulers on
pieces as shown.

Step 10. With the 3" x 18" ruler held in position, cut two strips from each fabric 2" x 11" as shown in Figure 8. Separate the strips into two groups: right sides facing up and right sides facing down. Seam two right-sides-up sets and gently press seams open; repeat with two right-sides-down sets as shown in Figure 9.

Figure 8
Cut 2"-wide strips.

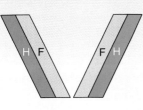

Figure 9
Lay pieces as shown.

Step 11. From one set, position the BiRangle ruler so that its diagonal line is aligned with the open seam. Cut the first two sides for a 1 3/4" x 3" pieced rectangle as illustrated by the two dashed cutting lines on Figure 10. Repeat and cut three more pieced rectangles from a matching set to make a total of six rectangles. ***Note: If using template, sew F to H and FR to HR to make F-H units.***

Step 12. Sew an F-H rectangle to the left side of the blocks made in Step 6 as shown in Figure 11.

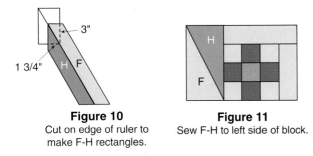

Figure 10
Cut on edge of ruler to make F-H rectangles.

Figure 11
Sew F-H to left side of block.

Step 13. Repeat the same two-step cutting process, and cut a total of six 1 3/4" x 3" pieced rectangles from the other two matching sets; set units aside.

Step 14. Layer G and I pieces right sides together. With the 3" x 18" ruler, cut two 1 1/2" x 8 1/2" 45-degree bias strips from each piece as shown in Figure 12.

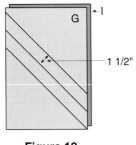

Figure 12
Cut 1 1/2"-wide strips at a 45-degree angle.

Step 15. Layer G and I with right sides together, and sew to make one G-I bias set; repeat to make two sets. Press seams open. Using the Baby Bias Square 4" ruler and open seams as cutting guides, cut three 1 1/2" x

Floral Bouquet
Placement Diagram
13" x 17 1/4"

1 1/2" G-I bias squares from each set for a total of six bias squares as shown in Figure 13. ***Note: If you do not have the Baby Bias Square, cut 1 1/2" x 1 1/2" squares using a ruler or make a template.***

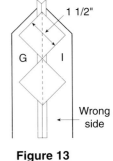

Figure 13
Cut 1 1/2" squares from the pieced bias strip.

Step 16. Sew one bias square to the end of one pieced rectangle made in Step 11 to make one set as shown in Figure 14; repeat for six sets. Press seams open.

Step 17. Sew one set to the right side of one unit made in Step 12 as shown in Figure 15, matching seams to complete one block; repeat for six blocks.

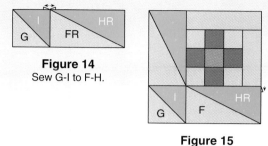

Figure 14
Sew G-I to F-H.

Figure 15
Sew units to complete block.

Step 18. Press blocks on both sides; square up to 3 1/2" x 3 1/2" if necessary.

Step 19. Stack the two J squares; cut in half twice on the diagonal to make eight J setting triangles; set aside two triangles.

Assembly

Step 1. Arrange the six pieced blocks with two K squares and six J triangles in four diagonal rows as shown in Figure 16. Join in rows; join rows to complete top.

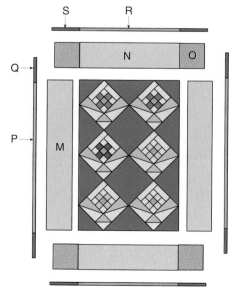

Figure 16
Arrange blocks with J, K and L in diagonal rows.

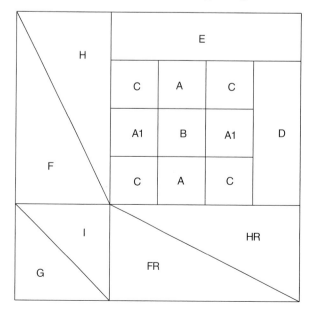

Figure 17
Sew border strips to pieced top.

Step 2. Stack the two L squares; cut in half on one diagonal to make corner triangles. Sew to the quilt top corners; press.

Step 3. Press top on both sides; square up edges if necessary.

Step 4. Referring to Figure 17, sew M strips to long sides of quilt top; press seams toward border. Sew two O squares to ends of each N strip; press seams open. Sew a strip to the top and bottom of the quilt top; press seams toward border.

Step 5. Mark quilting design and prepare for quilting referring to General Instructions.

Step 6. Sew a Q binding strip to each end of one P binding strip; repeat. Press seams open. Sew to long sides of quilt top.

Step 7. Sew an S binding strip to each end of one R binding strip; repeat. Press seams open. Sew to top and bottom of quilt top.

Step 8. Finish binding edges referring to General Instructions.

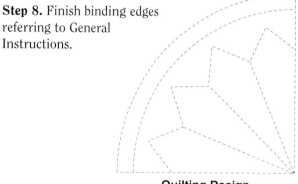

Quilting Design

Nine-Patch Floral Bouquet
3" x 3" Block
(Actual Size)

37

Decorating With Nine-Patch

Quilters love to decorate with quilts or quilted items in every room of the house. In this chapter you will find projects for the kitchen, bathroom, bedroom, living room and more. They may be pieced or appliquéd and range in size from a place mat to bed-size quilts. There are several projects that can be made in an afternoon and others that might take a few weeks.

Decorate your home with beautiful, eye-catching accessories using your sewing and quilting talents.

Dresser Scarf & Treasure Box

By Janice McKee

Making patchwork treasure boxes is fun and easy. Make a matching dresser scarf to decorate your bureau. Fill the box with jewelry or other small treasures.

Preparing Pieced Blocks

Step 1. Prepare templates using pattern pieces given (pages 42 and 48). Cut as directed on each piece. Referring to Figure 1, piece one block; repeat for three blocks.

Step 2. For box top, center the 8" square of batting on the wrong side of the 8" backing square. Place one pieced block right side up on batting.

Step 3. Hand-quilt the block using black quilting thread referring to Figure 2 for quilting suggestions.

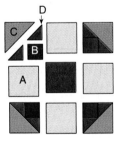

Figure 1
Piece block as shown.

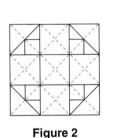

Figure 2
Hand-quilt block as shown.

Step 4. When quilting is complete, trim batting and backing to extend 1/4" all around block.

Step 5. Cut four strips black print 1" x 7"; stitch a strip to opposite sides; trim excess. Stitch remaining strips to remaining sides, butting corners; trim excess.

Step 6. Press raw edges under, making a 1/4" border around quilted block. Quilt in the ditch of the border. Set aside for box top. The remaining two blocks are for the dresser scarf.

Dresser Scarf

Step 1. Cut one square burgundy solid 9" x 9" and two squares 5 1/4" x 5 1/4". Cut each 5 1/4" square in half on one diagonal to make triangles.

Project Specifications

Dresser Scarf Size: 12 1/2" x 32"
Box Size: 6 1/2" x 6 1/2" x 4" sloping to 3"
Block Size: 6" x 6"
Number of Blocks: 3 pieced and 1 appliquéd

Materials

- 1 yard black print
- 1/3 yard burgundy solid
- 1/4 yard each tan, light gold and red prints
- 2 1/2" x 6" piece black solid
- 5" square rag rug or rope print for vase
- 1 piece low-loft batting 16" x 35" for dresser scarf
- 1 piece batting 22" x 22" for box
- 1 piece batting 8" x 8" for box top
- Backing piece 8" x 8" for box top
- 1 spool black all-purpose thread
- 1 spool each red and black quilting thread
- 1 skein each black and red 6-strand embroidery floss
- 1/2 yard fusible transfer web
- 1 red 1"-diameter wooden bead
- 1 yard 1/8"-wide red satin ribbon
- Basic sewing supplies and tools, glue stick, masking tape, stiff cardboard and freezer paper

Step 2. Sew a triangle to two adjacent sides of a pieced block as shown in Figure 3; repeat for second block.

Step 3. Join the two pieced sections with the 9" square as shown in Figure 4; press seams toward square.

Step 4. Prepare templates for appliqué pieces. Reverse shapes and trace on paper side of fusible transfer web. Cut around shapes, but not on the line. Fuse paper pieces to fabrics as directed on each piece for color.

Step 5. Cut out shapes along lines; remove paper.

Figure 3
Sew a triangle to 2 adjacent
sides of 1 block.

Figure 4
Sew the square between 2 blocks.

Step 6. Fuse pieces in place in the center of the burgundy square following manufacturer's instructions and referring to the Placement Diagram for arrangement.

Step 7. Using 2 strands of black floss, work buttonhole stitch around tulip petals and vase; work buttonhole stitch in red around leaves, stem and heart shape.

Step 8. Mark completed top in a diagonal 2" grid, leaving flower and vase shapes free to be outline-quilted.

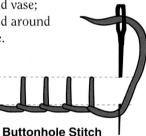

Buttonhole Stitch

Step 9. Cut a piece of backing from black print 18" x 37". Place right side down on flat surface; place 16" x 35" batting piece on top. Place marked top on batting; pin or baste layers together.

Step 10. Using black quilting thread, quilt on marked lines on background; quilt pieced blocks as shown in Figure 2.

Figure 5
Trim batting 2" beyond pieced section; trim
backing 2 1/2" beyond batting.

Step 11. When quilting is complete, trim *batting only* to extend 2" on all sides of quilt top. Trim backing piece to extend 2 1/2" all around batting as shown in Figure 5.

Step 12. Press edge of backing piece over 1/4" all around. Fold backing piece over batting to pieced section, mitering corners to make a border 2" wide all around. Slipstitch backing/border in place.

Step 13. Mark 1" away from edge on all sides; quilt on line with red quilting thread.

Step 14. With 2 strands of red floss, weave under every quilt stitch, forming a heavier line for trim.

Woven Stitch

Treasure Box

Step 1. Cut the following pieces from stiff cardboard: 6 1/2" x 6 1/2" for top; 6 1/4" x 6 1/4" for bottom; 3" x 6 1/4" for front side; 6 1/4" x 4" for backside; two pieces 6 1/2" x 4" wide at one end and 3" wide at the other are for remaining sides. Cut the same-size pieces from freezer paper and batting. ***Note:** Cutting is easy using an old blade in your rotary cutter or using a utility knife.*

Step 2. Cover both sides of cardboard box bottom and box side pieces with batting using the glue stick. Cover one side of cardboard box top with batting.

Step 3. Cut a piece of black print the size of the box bottom plus 1" all around. Bring raw edges of fabric piece up over the top; stitch securely to batting so that the fabric-covered side (which is the outside of the box bottom) is snug and smooth.

Step 4. Cut a piece of black print that extends 1/4" all around the freezer-paper piece for the box bottom for inside lining. Place freezer paper, shiny side up, on wrong side of fabric. Fold raw edges of fabric over paper; press on top of freezer paper.

Step 5. Place fabric-covered paper on batting side of box bottom to form lining. Whipstitch on three sides and remove paper; stitch remaining side.

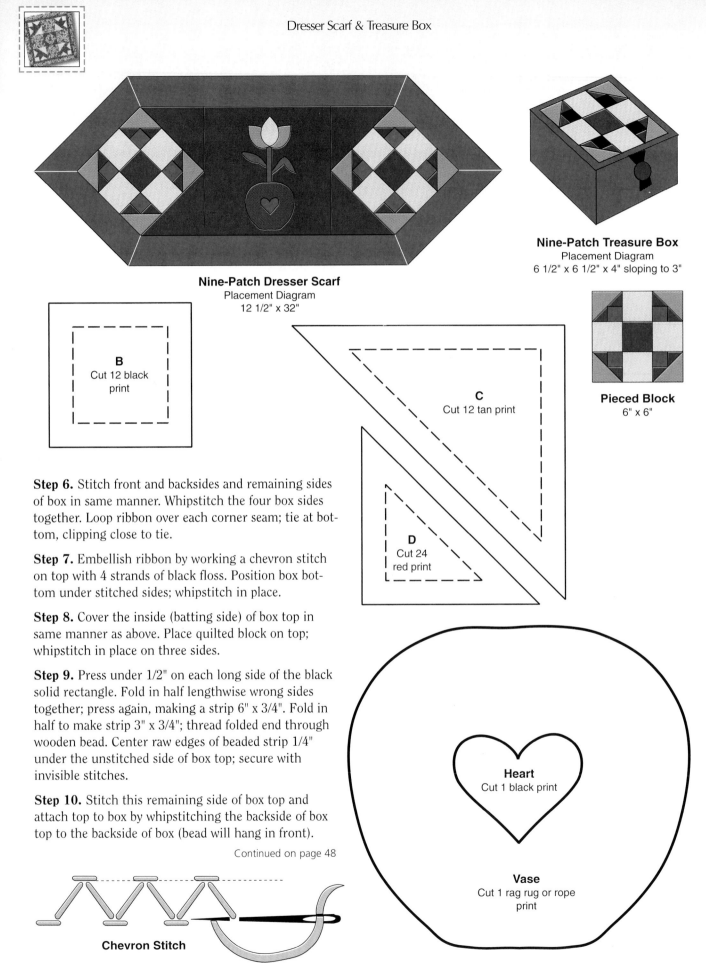

Nine-Patch Dresser Scarf
Placement Diagram
12 1/2" x 32"

Nine-Patch Treasure Box
Placement Diagram
6 1/2" x 6 1/2" x 4" sloping to 3"

Pieced Block
6" x 6"

B
Cut 12 black
print

C
Cut 12 tan print

D
Cut 24
red print

Heart
Cut 1 black print

Vase
Cut 1 rag rug or rope
print

Step 6. Stitch front and backsides and remaining sides of box in same manner. Whipstitch the four box sides together. Loop ribbon over each corner seam; tie at bottom, clipping close to tie.

Step 7. Embellish ribbon by working a chevron stitch on top with 4 strands of black floss. Position box bottom under stitched sides; whipstitch in place.

Step 8. Cover the inside (batting side) of box top in same manner as above. Place quilted block on top; whipstitch in place on three sides.

Step 9. Press under 1/2" on each long side of the black solid rectangle. Fold in half lengthwise wrong sides together; press again, making a strip 6" x 3/4". Fold in half to make strip 3" x 3/4"; thread folded end through wooden bead. Center raw edges of beaded strip 1/4" under the unstitched side of box top; secure with invisible stitches.

Step 10. Stitch this remaining side of box top and attach top to box by whipstitching the backside of box top to the backside of box (bead will hang in front).

Continued on page 48

Chevron Stitch

Birdhouse Place Setting

By Angie Wilhite

Make a simple Nine-Patch block to create a birdhouse for this quilted place mat with matching napkin. Machine appliqué accents the shapes to complete a neat table set.

Instructions

Step 1. Prewash all fabrics; do not use fabric softener.

Step 2. Cut napkin 13" x 13" from navy print. Press edges of napkin under 1/4" all around; press edges under 1/4" a second time. Stitch edges to hold.

Step 3. Apply fusible transfer web to wrong side of navy print and to a 4" x 6" piece red print. Trace bird pattern on red print and roof pattern on navy print. Draw a 1" x 5" shape on navy print for post. Cut out shapes; remove paper backing.

Step 4. Position bird on corner of napkin; fuse in place.

Step 5. Cut a piece of fabric stabilizer larger than the bird shape. Pin or baste stabilizer behind fused bird on wrong side of napkin. Satin-stitch around bird shape with matching thread. *Note: If using rayon thread for appliqué, thread top of machine with rayon and use all-purpose thread in the bobbin.* When stitching is complete, tear off fabric stabilizer; trim threads. Sew black button to bird's head as indicated on pattern.

Step 6. To make the Nine-Patch, cut three white print and three red strips 1 1/2" x 5". Sew white, red and white strips together; press seams. Sew red, white and red strips together; press seams. Cut a 1 1/2"-wide segment from the white-red-white strip and two 1 1/2" segments from the red-white-red strip.

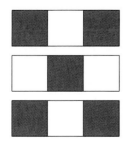

Figure 1
Join segments to make
Nine-Patch block.

Project Specifications

Skill Level: Beginner
Place Mat Size: 11" x 17"
Napkin Size: 12" x 12"

Materials

- 11" x 17" piece white solid
- 1/2 yard navy print
- 1/8 yard red print
- 6" x 6" piece white-on-white print
- 14" x 20" piece backing fabric
- 14" x 20" quilter's fleece
- 1/8" black button
- 3/8" white star button
- Rayon and all-purpose threads to match fabrics
- 1 spool nylon monofilament
- 1 package extra-wide, double-fold red bias tape
- 1/4 yard fusible transfer web
- 1/6 yard soft fusible interfacing
- 1/3 yard fabric stabilizer
- Fade-out pen
- Basic sewing supplies, tools and acrylic ruler

Step 7. Join the 1 1/2" segments to make a Nine-Patch block as shown in Figure 1; press.

Step 8. Cut a 3 1/2" x 3 1/2" piece each from fusible interfacing and fusible transfer web. Fuse the interfacing to the wrong side of the Nine-Patch block. Fuse the transfer web to the interfacing side of the Nine-Patch block; remove paper backing.

Step 9. Position Nine-Patch block, roof piece and 1" x 5" post piece on left side of 11" x 17" piece white referring to the Placement Diagram for arrangement; fuse in place. Pin or baste fabric stabilizer behind fused design. Satin-stitch around each shape using matching thread. Tear off fabric stabilizer; trim threads.

Step 10. Using fade-out pen and acrylic ruler, draw 1"-wide vertical lines on the place mat; do not draw lines through appliquéd shapes.

Step 11. Sandwich fleece between the backing piece and the appliquéd top. Thread top of machine with monofilament; use all-purpose thread in the bobbin. Machine-quilt on the drawn lines and in the ditch of the Nine-Patch block.

Step 12. Trim edges even; bind with red bias tape to finish edges.

Step 13. Sew white star button to center of Nine-Patch block.

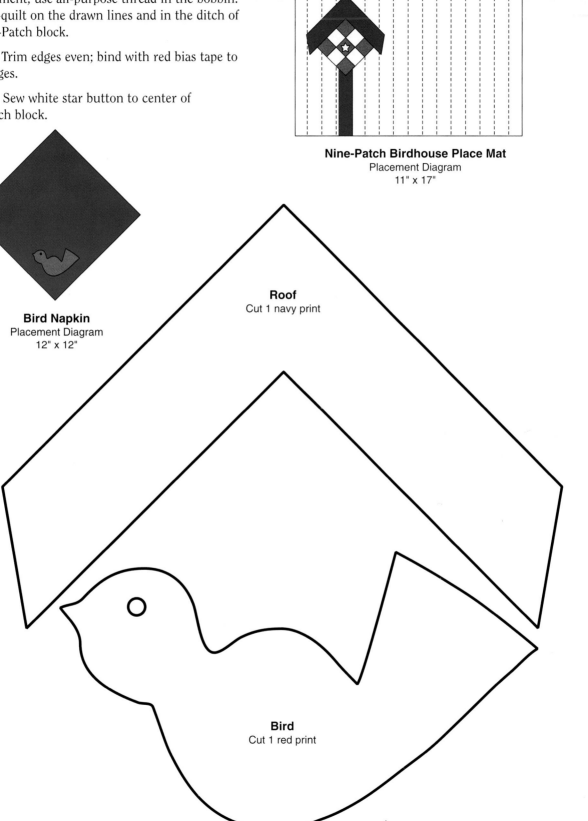

Nine-Patch Birdhouse Place Mat
Placement Diagram
11" x 17"

Bird Napkin
Placement Diagram
12" x 12"

Roof
Cut 1 navy print

Bird
Cut 1 red print

Starry Nine-Patch Pillows

By Ann Boyce

Combine plaids with maroon and beige solids and a coordinating print to create some pretty country-look accent pillows.

Instructions

Step 1. Cut three strips each maroon solid and beige-on-beige print 2" by fabric width. Sew a maroon to a beige to a maroon strip to make one strip set; press seams toward the maroon. Sew a beige to a maroon to a beige strip to make one strip set; press seams toward maroon.

Step 2. Cut each strip set into 2" segments referring to Figure 1.

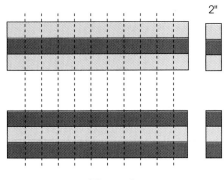

Figure 1
Cut strips into 2" segments.

Step 3. Join three segments as shown in Figure 2 to make a Nine-Patch block; repeat for eight blocks.

Step 4. Prepare templates for pieces A and B. Cut as directed on each piece.

Step 5. Join eight A pieces to make a star as shown in Figure 3; set in B pieces and Nine-Patch units referring to Figure 4 to complete one block. Press and repeat for a second block.

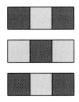

Figure 2
Join segments to make
Nine-Patch block.

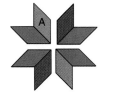

Figure 3
Join A pieces to make a star.

Project Specifications

Skill Level: Beginner
Pillow Size: 18 1/2" x 18 1/2"
Block Size: 13 1/2" x 13 1/2"
Number of Blocks: 2

Materials

- ✓ 1/2 yard beige-on-beige print
- ✓ 1/8 yard maroon solid
- ✓ 1/4 yard total red/beige plaids
- ✓ 1/2 yard red/beige print
- ✓ 1 1/8 yards backing fabric
- ✓ 2 (18") pillow forms
- ✓ Basic sewing supplies and tools, rotary cutter, ruler and cutting mat

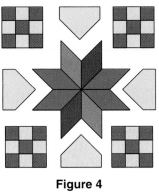

Figure 4
Join units to complete 1 block.

Step 6. Cut four strips 3" x 14" red/beige print; sew a strip to opposite sides of each pieced block. Press seams toward strips. Cut four more strips 3" x 19"; sew to remaining sides of each pieced block. Press seams toward strips.

Step 7. Cut four backing pieces 15" x 19". Turn under edge of one 19" side 1/4" and 1/4" again for hem; stitch to hold in place (pieces will measure 14 1/2" x 19").

Step 8. Layer two hemmed pieces right sides up, overlapping one hemmed edge over the other 10" as shown in Figure 5.

Starry Nine-Patch Pillow
Placement Diagram
18 1/2" x 18 1/2"

4 1/2"   14 1/2"

Figure 5
Overlap hemmed pieces as shown.

Step 9. Place pieced pillow top right sides together with hemmed pieces; pin. Sew around outside edges. Clip curves and turn right side out through overlapped opening; insert pillow form. Repeat to finish second pillow.

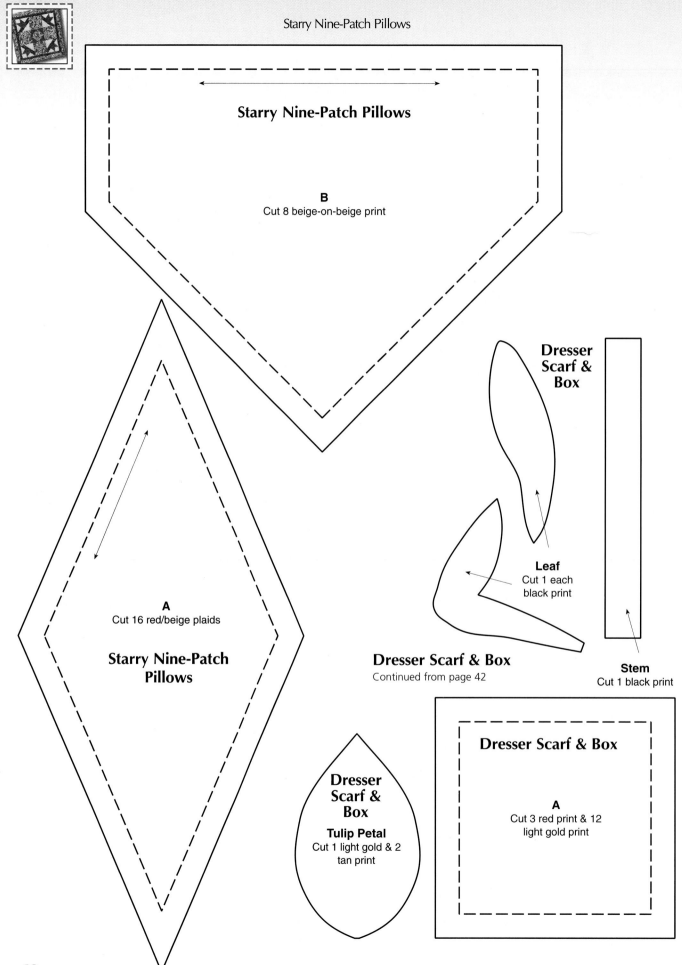

Starry Nine-Patch Pillows

B
Cut 8 beige-on-beige print

**Dresser
Scarf &
Box**

Leaf
Cut 1 each
black print

Stem
Cut 1 black print

A
Cut 16 red/beige plaids

**Starry Nine-Patch
Pillows**

Dresser Scarf & Box
Continued from page 42

**Dresser
Scarf &
Box**

Tulip Petal
Cut 1 light gold & 2
tan print

Dresser Scarf & Box

A
Cut 3 red print & 12
light gold print

Nine-Patch Bathroom Set

By Michele Crawford

Quilters like to decorate every room in the house—bathroom included. Use a simple Nine-Patch design to dress up your bath in colors to coordinate with your decor.

Instructions

Note: Use 1/4" seam allowance when sewing unless otherwise indicated. Sew pieces with right sides together, raw edges even using matching thread. Press seam allowances toward darkest fabric.

Towel & Curtain Tiebacks

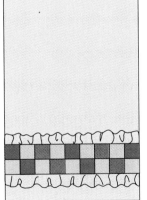

Towel
Placement Diagram
Size Varies

Step 1. Cut a 1 3/4" by fabric width strip from green, yellow, rose and yellow prints. Sew the strips together along length in that order; press. Cut into 1 3/4" segments.

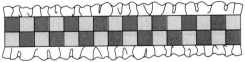

Curtain Tiebacks
Placement Diagram
2 1/2" x 20"

Step 2. For the towel border, join 1 3/4" segments as shown in Figure 1 to make a row; repeat. Join the two rows to make a checkerboard strip.

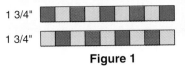

1 3/4"

1 3/4"

Figure 1
Make a checkerboard strip as shown.

Step 3. Cut two 11 1/2" pieces of lace. Center and sew one piece of lace on each side of the checkerboard strip; press.

Step 4. Center the strip across the towel; pin in place. Turn raw edges under 1/4" and slipstitch to the towel by hand. With monofilament in the top of the machine and gold thread in the bobbin, machine-quilt in the ditch of the seam between the strips and the lace on each side. ***Note:*** *Adjust the size of the checkerboard strip for a different size towel.*

Step 5. For the curtain tiebacks, join four 1 3/4" segments; repeat, offsetting as in Placement Diagram. Join the two rows to make a checkerboard strip.

Step 6. Cut two 20" pieces of lace. Center and sew a piece to each side of the strip. Cut two 3" x 20 1/2" strips yellow print for backing. Sew the pieced strip to the cut strip leaving ends open. Turn right side out; press. Turn raw edges on ends under 1/4"; slipstitch to close.

Seat Cover

Step 1. Prepare a template for piece G using pattern piece given for 12" x 12" block. Cut as directed on the piece. Cut two rose print squares 2 7/8" x 2 7/8"; cut on the diagonal of each square to make four E triangles. Cut four squares yellow print 4 1/2" x 4 1/2" for F and one square 3 3/8" x 3 3/8" for D. From muslin, cut four squares 1 7/8" x 1 7/8" for A, four 2 3/4" x 2 3/4" squares (cut each in half on the diagonal for B triangles) and two 3 1/2" x 3 1/2" squares (cut each in half on the diagonal for C triangles).

Toilet Seat Cover
Placement Diagram
Size Varies

Step 2. Sew E pieces to D; sew G to GR and set in B referring to Figure 2 for color placement; repeat. Set in A and sew to C; repeat for four units. Arrange pieced units with F in rows; join pieces in rows and press. Join rows; press.

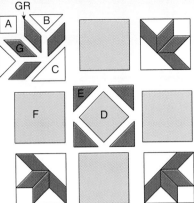

Figure 2
Join pieces to complete 1 block.

Step 3. Cut two 2 1/2" x 12 1/2" strips and two 2 1/2" x 16 1/2" strips green print. Sew a short strip to two opposite sides of the quilt block; press. Sew the longer strips to the top and bottom; press. Square should now measure 16 1/2" x 16 1/2".

Step 4. Cut a 16 1/2" x 16 1/2" square rose print for backing. Center a same-size piece of fleece on the wrong side of the backing piece; place pieced block wrong sides together with fleece. Pin layers together.

Step 5. Machine-quilt in the ditch of the seams. Hand-quilt 1/4" around outside of each flower shape in the muslin areas using the ecru quilting thread.

Step 6. Draw the outline of the toilet seat you wish to cover on paper. Add a 1/2" seam allowance around the outside edge. Center the pattern on the pieced and quilted square as shown in Figure 3. Pin; cut out.

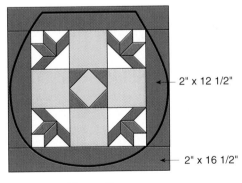

2" x 12 1/2"

2" x 16 1/2"

Figure 3
Center pattern on pieced block.

Step 7. Cut wide bias tape to fit across straight edge of cover; stitch to front. Fold bias tape over the seam allowance; hand-stitch to backing. Sew bias tape around the outside of the cover, turning under the ends 1/4". Fold bias tape over seam allowance; hand-stitch to the backing to form a casing.

Step 8. To make drawstring, cut a 50" piece of bias tape. Fold the bias tape in half; press and topstitch in place. Pin a small safety pin on one end of the bias tape; run through the casing. Remove the pin.

Step 9. Tie a knot in each end of the bias tape. Place the cover on the toilet lid, pull drawstring/tape tight around the cover and tie a bow to hold in place.

Tulip Unit for Toilet Tank Runner, Wall Quilt & Spare Roll Holder

Step 1. Prepare a template for piece G using pattern piece given for 18" x 18" block. Cut as directed on the piece.

Step 2. To make eight 6 1/2" pieced tulip sections, cut eight squares muslin 2 1/2" x 2 1/2" for A, eight squares muslin 3 3/4" x 3 3/4" (cut each in half on the diagonal for B triangles), and four squares muslin 4 7/8" x 4 7/8" (cut each in half on the diagonal for C triangles).

Step 3. Sew G to GR and set in B referring to Figure 2 for color placement; repeat. Set in A and sew to C; repeat for eight tulip units.

Toilet Tank Runner

Step 1. Join three tulip units all facing in the same direction as shown in Figure 4.

Figure 4
Join 3 tulip units.

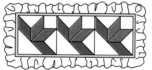

Toilet Tank Cover
Placement Diagram
6" x 18"

Step 2. Cut a 6 1/2" x 18 1/2" piece yellow print for backing. Center the same-size fleece piece on the wrong side of the backing piece. Center the pieced section on top of the fleece; pin layers together.

Step 3. Machine-quilt in the ditch of all seams. Hand-quilt 1/4" around the tulip shape in the muslin areas of each block. Topstitch around edge of runner piece 1/8" from edge.

Step 4. For the binding, cut two strips yellow print 2 1/4" by fabric width. Sew the ends together to make one long strip. Fold strip in half along length with wrong sides together; press.

Step 5. Pin binding to edges of runner with right sides together. Sew binding around edge, mitering corners

and overlapping ends. When stitching is complete, turn binding to backside; hand-stitch in place.

Step 6. Cut a 50" piece of lace. Sew the lace around the outside edges of the runner to finish.

Tulip Wall Quilt
Placement Diagram
23" x 23"

Wall Quilt

Step 1. Cut four squares yellow print 6 1/2" x 6 1/2" for F. Cut one square yellow print 4 3/4" x 4 3/4" for D. Cut two squares rose print 3 7/8" x 3 7/8" (cut each square on one diagonal to make E triangles).

Step 2. Sew an E triangle to each side of the D square. Arrange this unit with four tulip units and the F squares to make a block as shown in Figure 2.

Step 3. Cut four 1 1/2" x 18 1/2" strips green print and four squares 1 1/2" x 1 1/2" rose print. Sew a green print strip to two opposite sides of the pieced block; press. Sew a rose square to each end of the remaining two strips. Sew to remaining sides; press.

Step 4. Cur four 2" x 20 1/2" strips yellow print and four 2" x 2" squares rose print. Add to quilt sides as in Step 3.

Step 5. Cut a 25" x 25" square rose print for backing. Center the fleece on wrong side of square; center pieced section wrong sides together with fleece. Pin or baste layers together to hold flat.

Step 6. Machine-quilt in the ditch of the seams in center and borders. Hand-quilt 1/4" around each tulip in the muslin areas.

Step 7. Cut three strips 2 1/4" by fabric width yellow print. Sew the ends together to make one long strip. Fold strip in half along length with wrong sides together to make binding; press.

Step 8. Pin binding to edges of wall quilt with right sides together. Sew binding around edge, mitering corners and overlapping ends. When stitching is complete, turn binding to backside; hand-stitch in place.

Spare Roll Holder

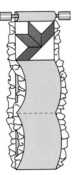

Step 1. Cut a 6 1/2" x 30" piece yellow print. Sew a pieced tulip unit to one end of the strip.

Step 2. Center the wrong side of the block strip from Step 1 on the 6 1/2" x 36 1/4" fleece. Pin; topstitch together.

Step 3. Cut two 36 3/4" pieces of lace. Turn ends under 1/4"; sew a piece of lace down each side of the block strip. Cut a 6 1/2" x 36 1/4" strip

Spare Roll Holder
Placement Diagram
6" x 21"

from yellow print for backing. Place right sides together with fleece and strip; stitch down each long side and across one end. Clip corners; trim excess, turn right side out.

Step 4. Hand-quilt 1/4" around the tulips in the muslin areas. Topstitch across the open end; topstitch down each long side 1/4" in with gold thread. Fold the straight bottom edge up to the bottom of the quilt block on the lining side. Pin and hand-stitch in place.

Step 5. Measure up 8" from the folded bottom; topstitch across.

Step 6. Cut a 2 1/4" x 6 1/2" strip yellow print. Press short ends under 1/4". Sew the strip across the top raw edge of the block. Press raw edge under 1/4".

Step 7. Fold strip over seam allowance; hand-stitch in place to make casing.

Step 8. Slide dowel through casing. Glue a wooden spool on each end of the dowel to finish.

Tulip
12" x 12" & 18" x 18" Blocks

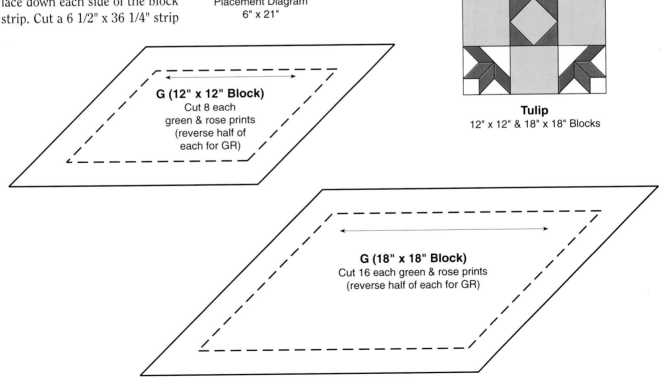

G (12" x 12" Block)
Cut 8 each
green & rose prints
(reverse half of
each for GR)

G (18" x 18" Block)
Cut 16 each green & rose prints
(reverse half of each for GR)

Seashore Stars

By Sherry Reis

Every quilt has its own story. Some are stitched to celebrate an occasion, some are created using a favorite fabric, and others are made for special people. This list of reasons goes on and on. The *Seashore Stars* and the *Ladders by the Sea* quilts came into being to clothe the twin antique beds at our summer home. Twenty light, medium and dark blue fabrics were used with bleached muslin for a scrap quilt look, but each quilt can also be created using as few as five fabrics.

Block A

Step 1. Cut 13 strips bleached muslin and 17 strips from medium blue fabrics 3 1/2" by fabric width.

Step 2. Stitch a medium blue strip to a muslin strip to a medium blue strip; press seams toward blue. Repeat for seven strip sets.

Step 3. Cut each strip set in 3 1/2" segments as shown in Figure 1—64 segments for blocks and 14 segments for borders. Set aside border segments.

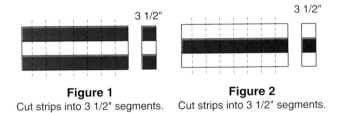

Figure 1
Cut strips into 3 1/2" segments.

Figure 2
Cut strips into 3 1/2" segments.

Step 4. From the remaining six muslin and three medium blue strips, sew a muslin strip to a medium blue strip to a muslin strip; press seams toward blue. Repeat for three strip sets.

Step 5. Cut each strip set in 3 1/2" segments as shown in Figure 2—32 segments are needed.

Step 6. Sew one segment made in Step 4 between two segments made in Step 2 to make Block A as shown in Figure 3; repeat for 32 A blocks.

Project Specifications

Quilt Size: 69" x 87"
Block Size: 9" x 9"
Number of Blocks: 17 Block C and 32 Block A

Materials

- 3 1/2 yards bleached muslin
- 3/4 yard total of 4 dark blue fabrics
- 2 yards total of 5 medium blue fabrics
- 3/4 yard total of 6 light/light blue fabrics
- 3/4 yard total of 5 medium/light blue fabrics
- Neutral color all-purpose thread
- Backing 73" x 91"
- Batting 73" x 91"
- Quilting thread
- 9 1/4 yards self-made or purchased binding
- Basic sewing supplies and tools

Figure 3
Join segments to make Block A.

Block B

Step 1. Cut four strips bleached muslin 9 1/2" by fabric width. Cut each strip into 9 1/2" segments for Block B. You will need 14 B blocks.

Block C

Step 1. Cut nine strips each light/light blue and the medium/light blue 2" by fabric width.

Step 2. Sew a medium/light blue fabric strip to a light/light blue strip; press seam allowance to the medium/light strip. Repeat for nine strip units.

Step 3. Cut strip units into 2" segments as shown in Figure 4—170 segments are needed.

Step 4. Join two of these segments to make a Four-Patch unit as shown in Figure 5; repeat for 85 units.

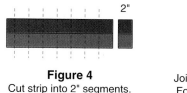

Figure 4
Cut strip into 2" segments.

Figure 5
Join units to make
Four-Patch units.

Step 5. Prepare templates for pieces A and B using pattern pieces given. To trim A, flip the B template onto the A template as shown in Figure 6, matching the finished seam lines and beginning and ending points. Trim excess on A piece. Repeat for right side, trimming top corner only. Trim fabric pieces accordingly. This eliminates any question of where to position fabric pieces before stitching (stitch left sides first).

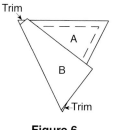

Figure 6
Place the B template on the
A template; trim as shown.

Step 6. Cut four strips bleached muslin 3 1/2" by fabric width. Using the trimmed A template, cut 68 units from the strips referring to Figure 7 (each strip will yield 21 units).

Figure 7
Place A template on 3 1/2"-wide strip; cut as shown.

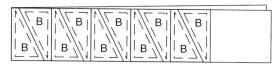

Figure 8
Cut B pieces from 3 1/2"-wide folded strips as shown.

Step 7. Cut four strips from dark blue fabrics 3 1/2" by fabric width. Fold strips wrong sides together to make a double layer 3 1/2" by half of fabric width. Using the B

template, cut 136 units from these strips as shown in Figure 8 (each strip yields 36 units). *Note: By cutting the B units from the folded strips, you will have both mirror-image units with each cut, cutting B and BR at the same time.*

Step 8. Sew a dark blue B and BR piece to each side of a muslin A piece as shown in Figure 9; press seam allowance toward B. Repeat for 68 units.

Step 9. Join five Four-Patch units with four A-B units to make Block C as shown in Figure 10; repeat for 17 blocks.

Figure 9
Sew B and BR to A.

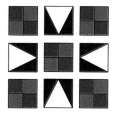

Figure 10
Join units to make Block C.

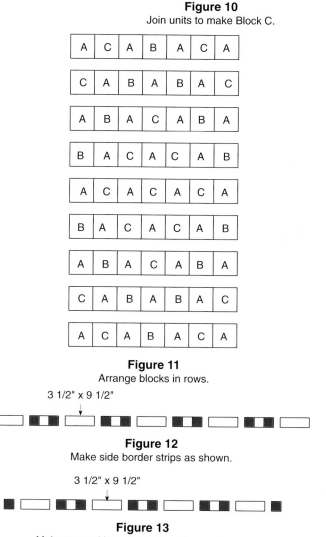

Figure 11
Arrange blocks in rows.

3 1/2" x 9 1/2"

Figure 12
Make side border strips as shown.

3 1/2" x 9 1/2"

Figure 13
Make top and bottom border strips as shown.

Quilt Top Assembly & Finishing

Step 1. Arrange A, B and C blocks in rows referring to Figure 11. Join the blocks in rows; join rows to complete pieced center; press.

Step 2. Cut five strips bleached muslin 3 1/2" by width of fabric. Cut strips into 9 1/2" segments. Using four of the 14 units set aside for borders from making Block A and the 3 1/2" x 9 1/2" muslin rectangles, piece two side border strips as shown in Figure 12.

Step 3. Cut one 3 1/2" x 3 1/2" square from four of the five medium blue fabrics for corner squares. Piece two strips using three of the 14 units set aside for borders and four 3 1/2" x 9 1/2" muslin rectangles; add a square to each end for top and bottom as shown in Figure 13. Sew strips to quilt; press seams toward border strips.

Step 4. Prepare top for quilting and finish referring to the General Instructions.

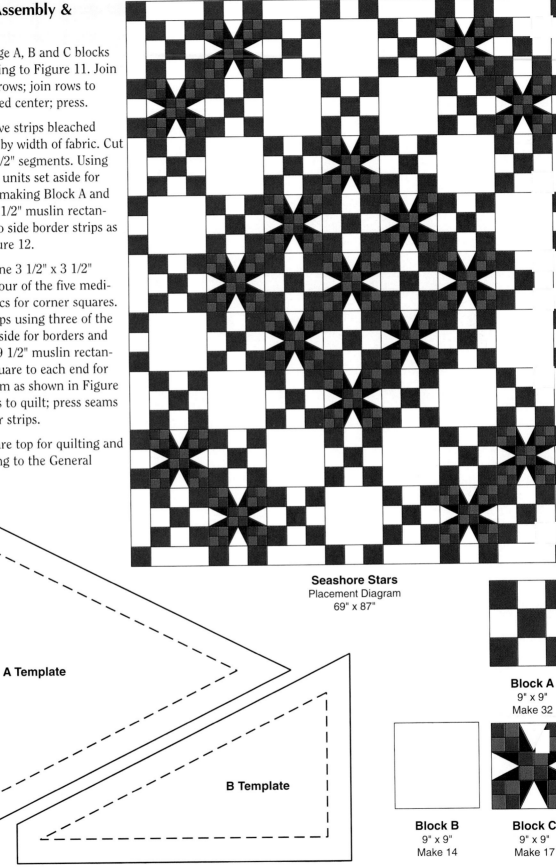

Seashore Stars
Placement Diagram
69" x 87"

Block A
9" x 9"
Make 32

A Template

B Template

Block B
9" x 9"
Make 14

Block C
9" x 9"
Make 17

Ladders by the Sea

By Sherry Reis

The *Ladders by the Sea* quilt matches the *Seashore Stars* quilt shown on page 54. Using the same basic methods and fabrics, a different yet coordinated design is formed.

Block A

Step 1. Create 32 A blocks referring to Steps 1–6 of *Seashore Stars* on page 55. Set aside blocks.

Block B

Step 1. Cut four strips bleached muslin 9 1/2" by fabric width. Cut into 9 1/2" segments for Block B. You will need 14 of these squares.

Four-Patch Units

Step 1. Cut nine strips each light/light blue and the medium/light blue 2" by fabric width.

Step 2. Stitch one light/light blue strip to each of the medium/light blue strips; press seams to the medium/light blue.

Step 3. Cut strip units into 2" segments; repeat for 170 segments (each strip should yield 21 segments).

Step 4. Pair the above units to form 85 Four-Patch units and stitch as shown in Figure 1. Five of these units will be needed for each of the C through G blocks.

Figure 1
Make Four-Patch units.

Blocks C & D

Step 1. Cut three strips each bleached muslin and dark blue 3 7/8" by fabric width. Cut each strip into 3 7/8" segments. Cut each segment in half on one diagonal to make triangles.

Figure 2
Make 56 units as shown.

Project Specifications

Skill Level: Beginner
Quilt Size: 69" x 87"
Block Size: 9" x 9"
Number of Blocks: 49 (a combination of 6 different pieced blocks)

Materials

- 3 1/2 yards bleached muslin
- 3/4 yard total of 4 dark blue fabrics
- 2 yards total of medium blue fabrics
- 3/4 yard total of 6 light/light blue fabrics
- 3/4 yard total of 5 medium/light blue fabrics
- Neutral color all-purpose thread
- Backing 74" x 91"
- Batting 74" x 91"
- Quilting thread
- 9 1/4 yards self-made or purchased binding
- Basic sewing supplies and tools

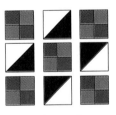

Figure 3
Join Four-Patch units and pieced triangle units to make Block C; repeat for 6 blocks.

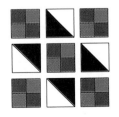

Figure 4
Join Four-Patch units and pieced triangle units to make Block D; repeat for 6 blocks.

Block A
9" x 9"
Make 32

Block B
9" x 9"
Make 14

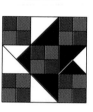

Block C
9" x 9"
Make 6

Block D
9" x 9"
Make 6

Block E
9" x 9"
Make 2

Block F
9" x 9"
Make 2

Block G
9" x 9"
Make 1

Ladders by the Sea
Placement Diagram
69" x 87"

Step 2. Sew a muslin triangle to a dark blue triangle to make a triangle/square unit as shown in Figure 2; repeat for 56 units. Set aside eight units for E and F blocks.

Step 3. Arrange four triangle/squares with five Four-Patch units in rows to make Block C as shown in Figure 3; repeat for six blocks.

Step 4. Arrange four triangle/squares with five Four-Patch units in rows to make Block D as shown in Figure 4; repeat for six blocks. Set aside.

Blocks E, F & G

Step 1. Cut three squares bleached muslin 4 1/4" x 4 1/4". Cut on both diagonals as shown in Figure 5. From three of the four dark blue fabrics, cut one square

Figure 5
Cut 4 1/4" square in half
on both diagonals.

each 4 1/4" x 4 1/4"; cut on both diagonals of each square for X, Y and Z triangles.

Step 2. Join the colored triangles with the muslin triangles to create two Z, four X and six Y units as shown in Figure 6.

Step 3. Cut one strip each bleached muslin and dark blue 3 7/8" by fabric width. Cut strips into 3 7/8" seg-

60

ments. Cut each segment in half on one diagonal to make triangles.

Make 4   Make 6   Make 2

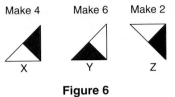

X   Y   Z

Figure 6
Complete X, Y and Z units as shown.

Step 4. Arrange the X, Y and Z units with the muslin and dark blue triangles and Four-Patch units to make Blocks E, F and G referring to Figures 7–9. Complete two blocks each E and F and one Block G.

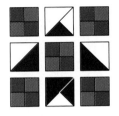

Figure 7
Piece Block E as shown;
repeat for 2 blocks.

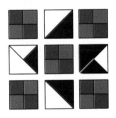

Figure 8
Piece Block F as shown;
repeat for 2 blocks.

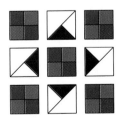

Figure 9
Piece 1 Block G as shown.

Quilt Top Assembly & Finishing

Step 1. Arrange A, B, C, D, E, F and G blocks in rows referring to Figure 10. Join the blocks in rows; join rows to complete pieced center; press.

Step 2. Cut five strips bleached muslin 3 1/2" by width of fabric. Cut strips into 9 1/2" segments. Using four of the 14 units set aside for borders from making Block A and the 3 1/2" x 9 1/2" muslin rectangles, piece two side border strips as shown in Figure 11.

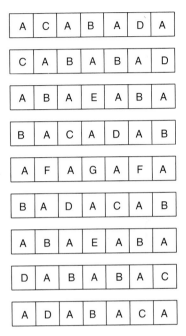

A	C	A	B	A	D	A
C	A	B	A	B	A	D
A	B	A	E	A	B	A
B	A	C	A	D	A	B
A	F	A	G	A	F	A
B	A	D	A	C	A	B
A	B	A	E	A	B	A
D	A	B	A	B	A	C
A	D	A	B	A	C	A

Figure 10
Arrange pieced blocks in rows as shown.

3 1/2" x 9 1/2"

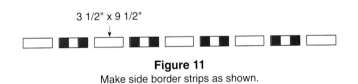

Figure 11
Make side border strips as shown.

Step 3. Cut one 3 1/2" x 3 1/2" square from four of the five medium blue fabrics for corner squares. Piece two strips using three of the 14 units set aside for borders and four 3 1/2" x 9 1/2" muslin rectangles; add a square to each end for top and bottom as shown in Figure 12. Sew strips to quilt; press seams toward border strips.

3 1/2" x 9 1/2"

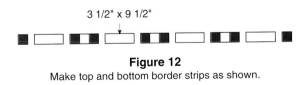

Figure 12
Make top and bottom border strips as shown.

Step 4. Prepare top for quilting and finish referring to General Instructions.

Welcome Banner

By Marian Shenk

If you are lucky enough to have an entrance hall to welcome visitors, this *Welcome Banner* would convey the message of warmth to all as they enter your home. It will probably bring many compliments to its maker as well.

Instructions

Step 1. Cut a square white-on-white print 18 1/2" x 18 1/2" for center. Fold and crease to mark center.

Step 2. Cut a green-on-green print circle 18" in diameter. Fold and crease to mark center.

Step 3. Transfer full-size appliqué design and letters to circle using a water-erasable marker or pencil and using center crease lines as guides for placement.

Step 4. Prepare patterns for each appliqué shape using full-size patterns given. Cut as directed on each piece, adding seam allowance when cutting.

Step 5. Pin and appliqué pieces in place on circle in numerical order referring to Figure 1 and using traced

Project Specifications

Skill Level: Intermediate
Banner Size: 31" x 31"
Block Size: 4 1/2" x 4 1/2"
Number of Blocks: 20

Materials

- 1 yard light green-on-green print
- 1/4 yard pink print
- 1/2 yard white-on-white print
- 1/8 yard dark green solid
- 1/3 yard burgundy print
- 1/3 yard medium green solid
- Scraps blue solid, blue print and mauve solid
- Backing 35" x 35"
- Batting 35" x 35"
- Coordinating all-purpose thread
- 1 spool off-white quilting thread
- 1 package 1/2"-wide light green bias tape
- 4 yards self-made or purchased dark green binding
- Basic sewing supplies and tools

lines as guides for placement and using matching threads for appliqué.

Step 6. When appliqué is complete, center circle on white-on-white square. Appliqué in place with 1/2"-wide light green bias tape covering edge of circle. Carefully trim away white-on-white layer under green circle leaving a 1/4" seam allowance.

Step 7. Cut three strips each white-on-white print, green-on-green print and pink print 2" by fabric width. Cut each strip in half to make two lengths. Sew strips together in the following sequences: white to a pink to a white; pink to a green to a pink; green to a white to a green; pink to a white to a pink; green to a pink to a green; and white to a green to a white. Cut each stitched set into 2" segments.

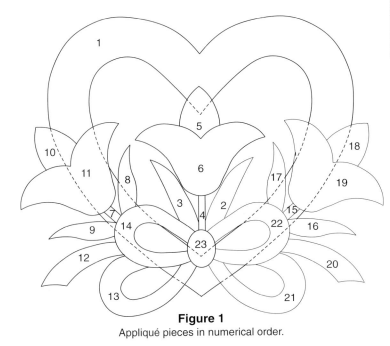

Figure 1
Appliqué pieces in numerical order.

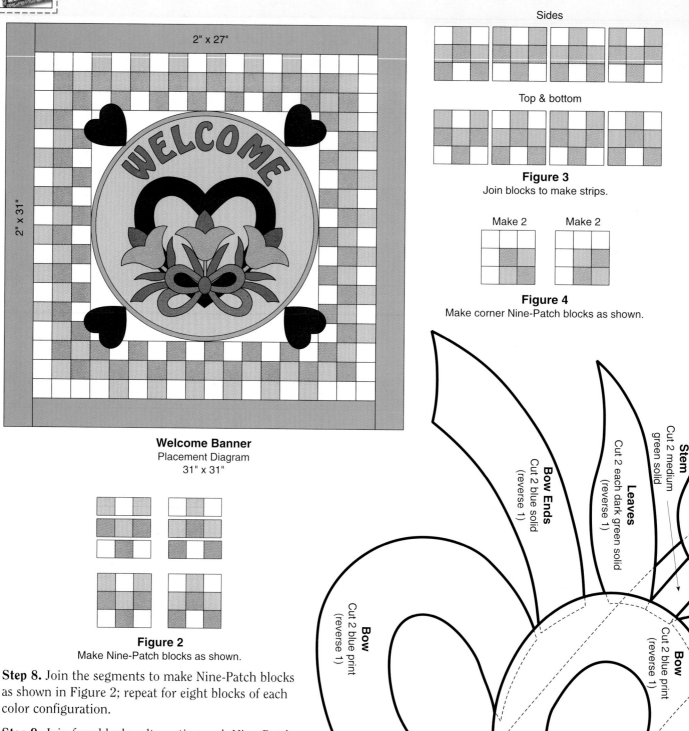

2" x 27"

2" x 31"

Welcome Banner
Placement Diagram
31" x 31"

Sides

Top & bottom

Figure 3
Join blocks to make strips.

Make 2   Make 2

Figure 4
Make corner Nine-Patch blocks as shown.

Figure 2
Make Nine-Patch blocks as shown.

Step 8. Join the segments to make Nine-Patch blocks as shown in Figure 2; repeat for eight blocks of each color configuration.

Step 9. Join four blocks, alternating each Nine-Patch block to make a row as shown in Figure 3; repeat for two rows for top and bottom. Set aside.

Step 10. Join four blocks, alternating each Nine-Patch block to make a row as shown in Figure 3; repeat for two side rows. Sew a side row to two opposite sides of the appliquéd section.

Step 11. To make corner blocks, cut 20 white-on-white and eight each pink and green print squares 2" x 2".

Stem
Cut 2 medium green solid

Leaves
Cut 2 each dark green solid (reverse 1)

Bow Ends
Cut 2 blue solid (reverse 1)

Bow
Cut 2 blue print (reverse 1)

Bow
Cut 2 blue print (reverse 1)

Connect at dotted line.

Bow Center
Cut 1 blue solid

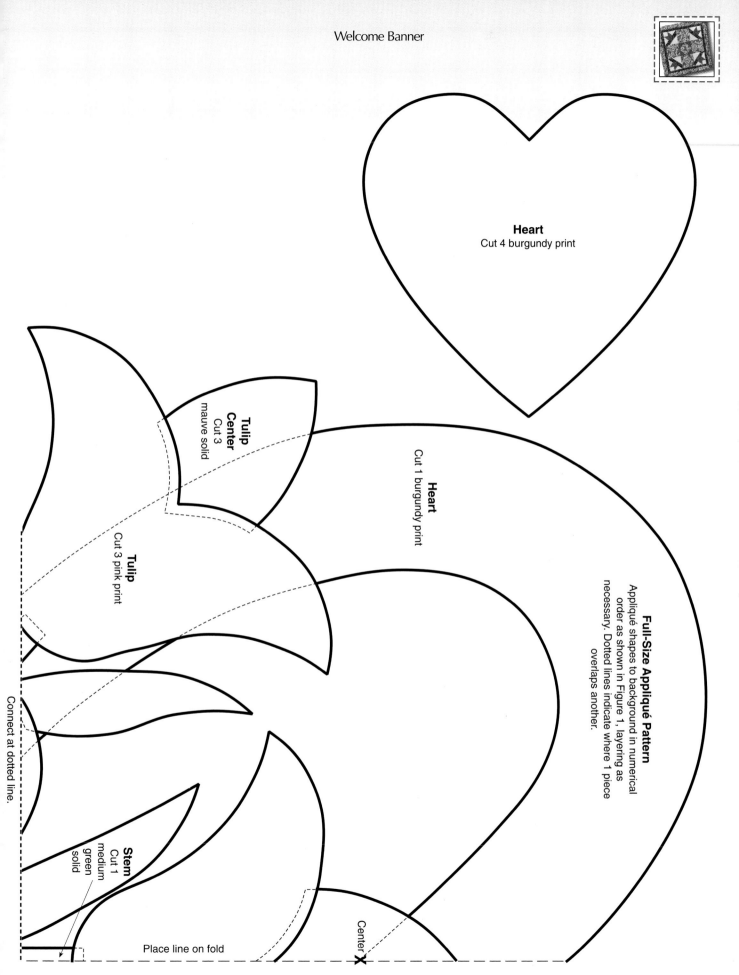

Heart
Cut 4 burgundy print

Tulip Center
Cut 3
mauve solid

Tulip
Cut 3 pink print

Heart
Cut 1 burgundy print

Full-Size Appliqué Pattern
Appliqué shapes to background in numerical order as shown in Figure 1, layering as necessary. Dotted lines indicate where 1 piece overlaps another.

Connect at dotted line.

Stem
Cut 1
medium
green
solid

Place line on fold

Center
X

Step 12. Join squares to make corner Nine-Patch blocks as shown in Figure 4; repeat for two blocks in each color configuration.

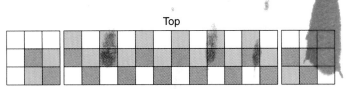

Top

Bottom

Figure 5
Sew a corner block to each end of a block row.

Step 13. Sew a corner block to each end of the remaining block rows as shown in Figure 5. Sew to the top and bottom of the appliquéd center. ***Note:*** *The stitched sample has one corner block turned in the wrong direction. The Placement Diagram shows correct placement.*

Step 14. Appliqué a heart shape in each corner of the center white square overlapping into border Nine-Patch blocks.

Step 15. Cut two strips medium green solid 2 1/2" x 27 1/2". Sew to top and bottom; press seams toward strips. Cut two more strips 2 1/2" x 31 1/2". Sew to remaining sides; press seams toward strips.

Step 16. Prepare top for quilting and finish referring to General Instructions.

Welcome Letters
Cut 1 each letter dark green solid

WEL
COME

Dolly & Me

By Beth Wheeler

Whip up a country-sweet lap quilt with matching doll quilt and coordinating window valance in your favorite colors! The doll quilt is an easy Nine-Patch—perfect for the young quilter. The lap quilt is a variation of a double Nine-Patch flowing from light-value to dark-value fabrics.

Project Notes

To achieve the subtle color motion in the lap quilt, choose 14 fabrics all in medium value. There should be some value variation between the lightest-value and darkest-value prints, but all should be low-contrast, medium-value prints to achieve this look. The instructions do not indicate the exact number of strips to cut for each fabric; rather, the drawings show the color configuration used to complete the sample. The number and color configuration varies with the number of fabrics used.

The lap quilt may be enlarged by adding columns and rows, but removing columns and rows to reduce the size will eliminate some of the blending effect.

The sample is a regimented arrangement of blending fabrics. Feel free to arrange your blocks in any configuration you desire. Play with the blocks on a flat surface, such as a bed, until you are pleased with the effect.

All fabrics should be washed, dried and pressed before construction. A 1/4" seam allowance is used throughout.

The batting in the doll quilt should be thinner than the batting in the lap quilt to avoid excessive bulk. Choose a thinner batting or split a thick one.

Adjust size of window valance by adding length to the valance. For a full, ruffled look, make the valance two times the width of the window. For the look of a cornice, the valance should be the width of the window, plus enough to wrap around the ends of the curtain rod. Valance may be adjusted on rod by shirring slightly.

Doll Quilt

Step 1. Cut three strips each 1 1/2" by fabric width from two fabrics. Cut each strip in half along length.

Project Specifications

Skill Level: Intermediate
Doll Quilt: 15" x 19"
Lap Quilt: 47" x 57"
Valance: 14" x 49"
Number of Blocks: Doll Quilt—12; Lap Quilt—180; Valance—24

Materials

- 5 yards fabric for sashing/borders
- 1/2 to 1 yard each 14 coordinating fabrics (see Project Notes)
- Backing 18" x 21" for doll quilt and 50" x 60" for lap quilt
- Batting 18" x 21" for doll quilt and 50" x 60" for lap quilt
- Neutral color all-purpose thread
- 1 spool clear monofilament
- 2 yards self-made or purchased binding for Doll Quilt and 6 1/2 yards for Lap Quilt
- Basic sewing supplies and tools

Sew two different strip sets as shown in Figure 1. Cut each set in 1 1/2" segments. Join segments to make six X and six O blocks as shown in Figure 2.

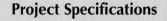

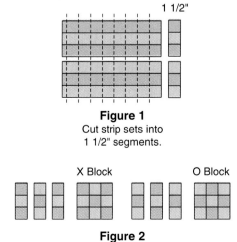

Figure 1
Cut strip sets into 1 1/2" segments.

X Block   O Block

Figure 2
Join segments to make Nine-Patch blocks as shown.

Step 2. Cut eight strips sashing fabric 1 1/2" x 3 1/2";

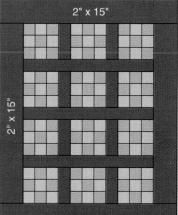

Dolly & Me Doll Quilt
Placement Diagram
15" x 19"

Dolly & Me Lap Quilt
Placement Diagram
47" x 57"

join three blocks with two strips to make one row. Repeat for four rows; press

Step 3. Cut three sashing strips 1 1/2" x 11 1/2"; join the rows with these strips.

Step 4. Cut four strips border fabric 2 1/2" x 15 1/2"; sew a strip to each long side and to the top and bottom. Press seams toward strips.

Step 5. Prepare top for quilting and finish referring to General Instructions.

Lap Quilt

Step 1. Cut several strips from each of the 14 fabrics 1 1/2" by fabric width. Label each fabric with a letter, number or name. ***Note:*** *Rather than pin an identification tag on each fabric, I cut a snip from each fabric while evening the ends and taped it to an index card or piece of typing paper. This*

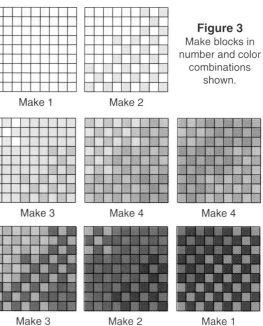

Figure 3
Make blocks in number and color combinations shown.

Make 1   Make 2

Make 3   Make 4   Make 4

Make 3   Make 2   Make 1

prevents nicks in the rotary blade when rolling over pins, and the index card can be pinned to a curtain beside the sewing machine for quick reference.

Step 2. Stitch strips together to make X and O blocks (180 blocks total) as for Doll Quilt. The first set will be fabrics 1 and 2; the next will be fabrics 2 and 3; 3 and 4; 4 and 5, etc. You will need fewer 1-2 and 13-14 blocks than the others. Refer to Figure 3 for coloration of blocks similar to sample quilt.

Step 3. Join X and O blocks to make rows containing three blocks each referring to Figure 4; repeat for three rows. Join the rows to make a larger block; repeat for 20 larger blocks, again referring to Figures 3 and 4 for coloration of blocks.

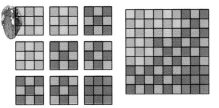

Figure 4
Join 9 Nine-Patch blocks to make a larger block.

1 1/2" x 9 1/2"

Figure 5
Join blocks with sashing strips to make a row.

1 1/2" x 9 1/2"

1 1/2" x 39 1/2"

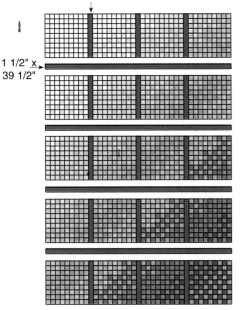

Figure 6
Join rows with sashing strips.

Step 4. Cut 15 strips sashing fabric 1 1/2" x 9 1/2".

Step 5. Stitch sashing strips between blocks to make a row as shown in Figure 5; repeat for five rows and press. ***Note:*** *Refer to the Placement Diagram and photo of sample to note pattern formed by placement of blocks.*

Step 6. Cut four strips sashing 1 1/2" x 39 1/2". Join rows with strips as shown in Figure 6; press.

Step 7. Cut two strips border fabric 4 1/2" x 49 1/2"; sew a strip to each long side. Press seams toward strips. Cut two more strips 4 1/2" x 47 1/2"; sew a strip to top and bottom. Press seams toward strips.

Dolly & Me Window Valance
Placement Diagram
14" x 49"

Step 8. Prepare top for quilting and finish referring to General Instructions.

Valance

Step 1. Make 12 each X and O blocks from three chosen fabrics using 1 1/2" strips as for Doll Quilt.

Step 2. Cut two strips each 1 1/2" x 8 1/2" and 1 1/2" x 47 1/2" and 22 strips 1 1/2" x 3 1/2" from sashing fabric. Cut one piece sashing fabric 20 1/2" x 49 1/2" for valance top and lining.

Step 3. Stitch 1 1/2" x 3 1/2" sashing strips between blocks, alternating X's and O's, to make a row with 12 blocks as shown in Figure 7; repeat. Join the rows

1 1/2" x 3 1/2"

Figure 7
Stitch sashing between X and O blocks to make rows.

1 1/2" x 47 1/2"

Figure 8
Stitch sashing between blocks and rows for valance.

Continued on page 75

Bedroom Ensemble

By Beth Wheeler

Personalize a special bedroom quickly and economically with touches of patchwork in colors to coordinate with existing paint or wallpaper. This ensemble can be completed in one weekend, depending on window and bed sizes.

Project Notes

Adjust size of window valance by positioning napkins farther apart or closer together, or add and reduce the number of napkin points to fit. Valance may be adjusted on rod by shirring slightly.

Making Nine-Patch Blocks

Step 1. Cut 12 strips each 2" by fabric width from pink check and blue-and-pink print.

Step 2. Stitch one blue-and-pink strip between two pink check strips to make a pink unit as shown in Figure 1; press seam allowances toward pink strips. Repeat for 4 sets.

Figure 1
Create a pink unit.

Step 3. Stitch one pink check strip between two blue-and-pink strips to make a blue unit as shown in Figure 2; press seam allowances toward pink strip. Repeat for 4 sets.

Figure 2
Create a blue unit.

Step 4. Cut 2" segments from each strip set as shown in Figure 3; join segments to make 25 O and 27 X units as shown in Figure 4.

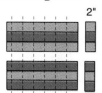

Figure 3
Cut 2" segments from each unit.

X Unit O Unit
Figure 4
Make X Unit and O Unit.

Project Specifications

Skill Level: Beginner
Sheet Size: 66" by any length
Pillowcase Size: 21 1/2" by any length
Valance Size: Approximately 12 1/2" x 45"
Table Scarf Size: 27 1/2" x 27 1/2"
Nine-Patch Size: 4 1/2" x 4 1/2"
Number of Blocks: 29 O units and 31 X units

Materials

- Pair of solid color pillowcases 21 1/2" by any length
- Solid-color sheet 66" wide by any length
- 5 (16"-square) table napkins
- 2 yards each pink check, blue-and-white print and blue plaid fabrics
- Neutral color all-purpose thread
- 1 spool clear monofilament
- Basic sewing supplies and tools

Pillowcase

Step 1. Cut one strip 2 1/2" by fabric width blue plaid. Cut eight 5" segments from the strip for sashing between blocks.

Step 2. Join three Nine-Patch units, alternating X and O units with four 2 1/2" x 5" segments to make a row; press. Repeat for second row.

Step 3. Cut two strips 3" x 22"; sew a strip to the top and bottom of each strip. Press seams toward strips. Pieced strip should measure 10" x 22".

Step 4. Join strips on both

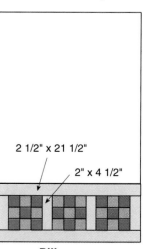

Pillowcase
Placement Diagram
21 1/2" by any length

2 1/2" x 21 1/2"

2" x 4 1/2"

ends to make a tube. Press under top and bottom edges 1/2" all around.

Step 5. Pin pieced section to pillowcase along bottom edge, lining up pressed seam edge with edge of pillowcase on the right side and matching end seams with pillowcase seam; hand- or machine-stitch pieced sections to pillowcase; press. **Note:** *Adjust the size of the sashing strips between blocks to fit different size pillowcases, if necessary.* Report for second pillowcase.

1 1/2" x 66"   1 1/2" x 4"

Sheet
Placement Diagram
66" by any length

X Unit
4 1/2" x 4 1/2"

O Unit
4 1/2" x 4 1/2"

Sheet

Step 1. Cut one strip 2" by fabric width blue plaid. Cut strip into 5" segments for sashing. You will need 12 segments, six X units and five O units to piece a 5" x 68" strip. **Note:** *Adjust the size of the sashing or add more blocks to fit a different size sheet, if necessary.*

Step 2. Join the sashing segments with the X and O units beginning and ending with a sashing segment. Refer to the Placement Diagram for arrangement of X and O units.

Step 3. Cut four strips blue plaid 2" by fabric width. Join two strips on one short end to make a long strip; repeat. Sew a strip to the top and bottom of the pieced section; trim excess at ends; press seam allowances toward plaid strips.

Step 4. Press outer edges of strip under 3/4". Pin border along hem edge of sheet.

Step 5. Hand- or machine-stitch strip in place on top edge of sheet to finish.

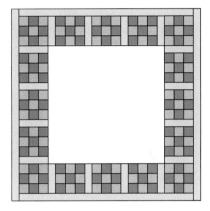

Table Scarf
Placement Diagram
27 1/2" x 27 1/2"

Table Scarf

Step 1. Cut two strips blue plaid 1" by fabric width. Cut strip into 5" segments; you will need 16 segments.

Step 2. Join two X units and one O unit with four strips to make a short row; press. Repeat for second row.

Step 3. Sew a strip to the top and bottom of a 16" napkin; press.

Step 4. Join two X units and three O units with four strips to make a long row; press. Repeat for second row.

Step 5. Sew a strip to opposite sides of the pieced center; press.

Step 6. Cut two strips 2" x 25" and two strips 2" x 28" blue plaid. Sew the 25" strips to the top and bottom and the 28" strips to opposite sides; press seams toward strips.

Step 7. Cut a blue plaid square the same size as the pieced front. Pin together, right sides facing.

Step 8. Stitch all around outside edges leaving an opening for turning. Clip corners; turn; press. Hand-stitch opening closed to finish.

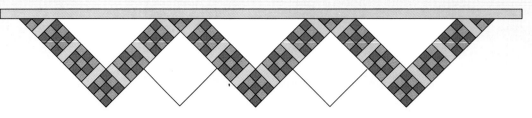

Valance
Placement Diagram
Approximately 12 1/2" x 45"

Valance

Step 1. Cut three napkins diagonally as shown in Figure 5; set three halves aside.

Figure 5
Cut napkins in half
diagonally.

Step 2. Cut three strips blue plaid 2 1/2" by fabric width. Cut strips into 5" segments. Join one X unit with two O units and three strips referring to Figure 6 for placement; press. Measure in 4 1/2" on two adjacent sides as shown in Figure 6. Lay pieced strip on napkin triangle right side down, again referring to Figure 6. Stitch along lower long edge of pieced strip; fold strip back even with edge of napkin and press. Trim excess even with napkin triangle at top edge, referring to Figure 7. Repeat for three pieced napkin triangles.

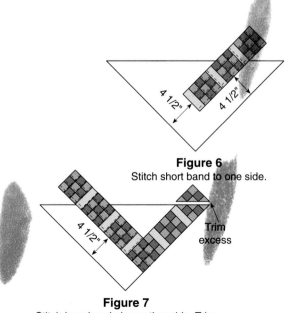

Figure 6
Stitch short band to one side.

Figure 7
Stitch long band along other side. Trim
excess even with unstitched edge.

Step 3. Join two O units with two X units and three strips to make a row; press. Place stitched strip on triangle 4 1/2" from edge referring to Figure 7. Stitch, fold and press as in Step 2. Trim excess even with napkin triangle at top edge. Repeat for three pieced napkin triangles.

Step 4. Place one plain napkin point (set aside in Step 1) on top of one pieced napkin point, right sides together. Stitch along point edges as shown in Figure 8. Turn; press. Repeat with remaining napkin pieces.

Step 5. Cut fourth napkin on the diagonal. Arrange pieced points with plain triangles on work surface as in Figure 9, overlapping more or less to fit desired window. Pin in place; stitch along raw edges.

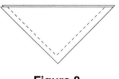

Figure 8
Stitch together along point edges.

Step 6. Cut four strips plaid 2 1/2" wide (or width of curtain rod plus 3/4") by window measurement for casing.

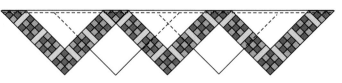

Figure 9
Arrange points on work surface,
overlapping pieced points with plain
triangles as shown; stitch across top edge.

Step 7. Stitch two strips together on short ends; repeat. Trim to size of window measurement. Stitch the two strips together along one long edge, right sides together; press seam allowance open.

Step 8. Open strips; pin one edge along top edge of valance, right sides together. Stitch together with a 1/4" seam allowance; fold strip up and press.

Step 9. Press remaining long raw edge under 1/4". Press and stitch a 1/2" hem on short ends.

Step 10. Fold pressed edge to wrong side of valance, enclosing raw edge on backside. Machine-stitch in place with a zigzag or blind-hem stitch using monofilament thread in the top of the machine and all-purpose thread in the bobbin; press to finish.

Dolly & Me
Continued from page 70

with a 1 1/2" x 47 1/2" strip as shown in Figure 8. Sew the remaining strip to the bottom of the pieced section; press.

Step 4. Sew the 1 1/2" x 8 1/2" sashing strips to each short end of the pieced section; press.

Step 5. Sew the 20 1/2" x 49 1/2" piece to the top of the pieced section; press. Fold the large strip right sides together over the pieced bottom section. Stitch around outside edges, leaving a 4" opening on one side to turn and a 1 1/2" opening from top edge on each side for curtain rod as shown in Figure 9. Turn right side out through opening; press.

Step 6. Hand-stitch turning opening closed.

Step 7. Measure 1 1/2" down from upper folded edge; mark a line across top. Stitch along line to make a casing to accommodate the curtain rod. *Note: The openings left when stitching in Step 5 remain open for insertion of rod.*

Folded edge

1 1/2"

4"

1 1/2"

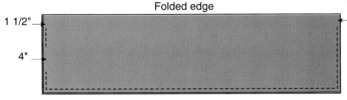

Figure 9
Stitch around valance, leaving openings, as indicated.

Glorious Nine-Patch Quilts

*N*o matter what size the bed, a Nine-Patch quilt will create a center-piece around which a room can be decorated. Quilts ranging in size from miniature to queen are found in this chapter, and all use quick and easy construction methods.

Whether you make one for yourself or others, the satisfaction of seeing your work displayed on a bed or on a wall is an awesome experience. Quilts are made to be used and shared.

Harbinger of Spring

By Lucy A. Fazely

When the tulips blossom summer can't be far behind. Fabric tulips blossom in many colors on this attractive Nine-Patch quilt. Plant your quilt garden inside this year with this pretty bed quilt.

To Make Blocks

Step 1. To make center square units, cut the following strips across the width of the fabric: three strips 3 3/8" yellow—cut into thirty 3 3/8" segments; and five strips 2 7/8" white-on-white—cut into sixty 2 7/8" segments.

Step 2. Cut each of the 2 7/8" x 2 7/8" white-on-white squares in half on the diagonal to make triangles.

Step 3. Sew a white-on-white triangle to each side of the 3 3/8" yellow squares as shown in Figure 1; repeat for 30 units.

Figure 1
Sew a white triangle to each
side of a 3 3/8" yellow square.

Step 4. To make the side squares, cut the following strips 4 1/2" by the width of the fabric: eight strips white-on-white and five strips each light and medium green.

Step 5. Using the template given, cut 120 A pieces from the 4 1/2" white-on-white strips as shown in Figure 2.

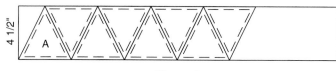

Figure 2
Use piece A to cut pieces from 4 1/2"-wide white-on-white strips.

Step 6. Cut 120 B pieces from right side of 4 1/2" medium green strips and 120 C pieces from right side of 4 1/2" light green strips.

Step 7. Piece 120 side squares using cut pieces as shown in Figure 3.

Project Specifications

Skill Level: Beginner
Project Size: 84" x 98"
Block Size: 12" x 12"
Number of Blocks: 30

Materials

- 1/2 yard yellow print
- 4 yards white-on-white print
- 1/8 yard each of 10 prints in spring tulip colors
- 2/3 yard light green
- 5 yards medium green
- 2 1/2 yards dark green for border
- Backing 88" x 100"
- Batting 88" x 100"
- All-purpose thread to match fabrics
- 1 spool each white and green quilting thread
- Yellow and green pearl cotton
- Basic sewing supplies and tools

Figure 3
Join pieces to make
side squares.

Step 8. To make corner squares, cut the following strips 2 1/2" by fabric width: one strip each of the 10 spring prints; 25 strips white-on-white; and eight strips medium green.

Step 9. Sew one of the 2 1/2"-wide strips of spring prints to a 2 1/2"-wide white-on-white strip along length; repeat for each spring print. Cut each stitched strip into 12 segments 2 1/2" wide as shown in Figure 4.

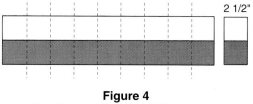

Figure 4
Cut stitched strips into 2 1/2" segments.

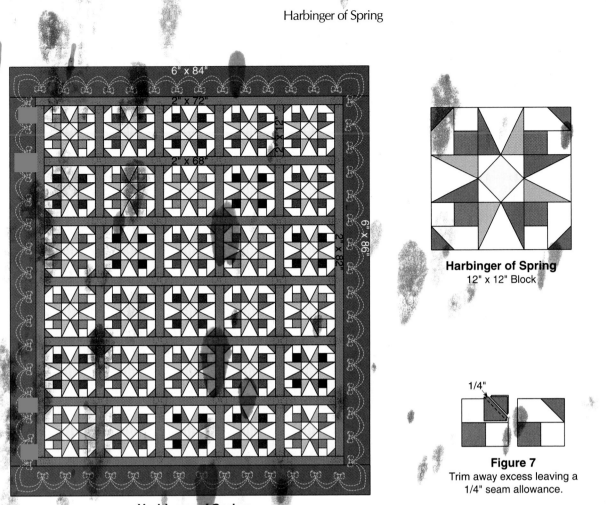

Harbinger of Spring
Placement Diagram
84" x 98"

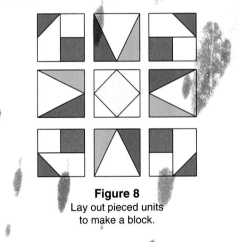

Harbinger of Spring
12" x 12" Block

Figure 7
Trim away excess leaving a
1/4" seam allowance.

Step 10. Cut the remaining 15 white-on-white strips into 120 rectangles each 2 1/2" x 4 1/2". Sew a white-on-white rectangle to each of the pieced rectangles referring to Figure 5.

Step 11. Cut the medium green strips into 120 segments 2 1/2" wide. Lay one 2 1/2" x 2 1/2" square over the end of a previously pieced white-on-white rectangle unit opposite the spring-colored print. Sew a diagonal line from corner to corner of the green square only as shown in Figure 6.

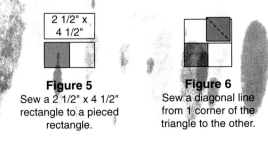

Figure 5
Sew a 2 1/2" x 4 1/2"
rectangle to a pieced
rectangle.

Figure 6
Sew a diagonal line
from 1 corner of the
triangle to the other.

Step 12. Trim away excess at corner to 1/4" seam allowance as shown in Figure 7; press seam toward green print. Repeat for 120 units.

Assembly

Step 1. Lay out pieced units to complete one block as shown in Figure 8. Join the units in rows; join the rows to complete the block; press. Repeat for 30 blocks.

Figure 8
Lay out pieced units
to make a block.

Step 2. Cut 26 strips 2 1/2" by fabric width medium green print. Cut eight of these strips into 24 short sashing strips 2 1/2" x 12 1/2" each. Use remaining strips for Steps 3–5. Join five blocks with four strips to make a horizontal row as shown in Figure 9; repeat for six rows. Press seams toward strips.

Step 3. Piece five strips 2 1/2" x 68 1/2" medium green print. Join the rows with the strips; press seams toward strips. ***Note:*** *Sashing and border strips will need to be pieced to the lengths given.*

2 1/2" x 12 1/2"

Figure 9
Join blocks and strips to make a horizontal row.

Step 4. Piece two strips 2 1/2" x 82 1/2" medium green; sew a strip to opposite sides of the pieced center. Press seams toward strips.

Step 5. Piece two strips 2 1/2" x 72 1/2" medium green; sew a strip to the top and bottom of the pieced center. Press seams toward strips.

Step 6. Cut nine strips dark green border print 6 1/2" by fabric width. Join together on short ends to make two strips 6 1/2" x 86 1/2" and two strips 6 1/2" x 84 1/2". Sew the longer strips to opposite sides and the shorter strips to the top and bottom of the pieced center; press seams toward strips.

Step 7. Mark borders and sashing with quilting designs given. Prepare top for quilting and finish referring to the General Instructions section. Quilt border design using yellow pearl cotton, leaves and flowers using green pearl cotton, in the ditch of block seams using white quilting thread and in the ditch of borders using green quilting thread referring to the Placement Diagram for arrangement.

Step 8. Finish edges with self-made binding using dark green border fabric referring to General Instructions.

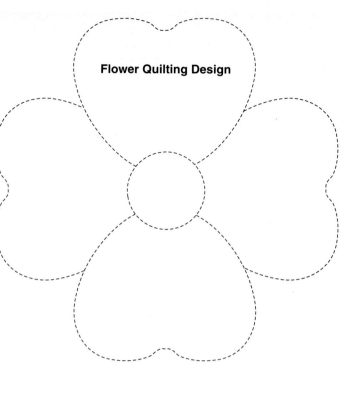

Flower Quilting Design

Border Quilting Design

Connect here

Leaf Quilting Design

B & C
Cut 120 medium green
print for B
Reverse & cut 120 light
green print for C

A
Cut 120 white-on-white print

Connect here

Center of corner

Miniature Nine-Patch

By Lucy A. Fazely

Delicate colors combine with small pieces to make this simple miniature wall quilt. Fine hand-quilting stitches accent the heart and curved quilting designs. Use this little quilt as a table centerpiece or as an accent for a small wall space.

Instructions

Note: A 1/4" seam allowance is included in all measurements given.

Step 1. Cut the following strips across the width of the fabric: one strip muslin 1 1/4"; four strips blue print 1 1/4"; two strips muslin 2 3/4".

Step 2. Make the following second cuts from the strips cut in Step 1: one piece blue print 1 1/4" x 8"; two strips blue print 1 1/4" x 15"; two strips muslin 1 1/4" x 8"; and one strip muslin 1 1/4" x 15".

Step 3. Stitch the cut strips together to form one 15" strip set and one 8" strip set as shown in Figures 1 and 2. Press seams toward darkest fabric.

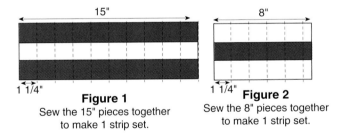

Figure 1
Sew the 15" pieces together to make 1 strip set.

Figure 2
Sew the 8" pieces together to make 1 strip set.

Step 4. Cut the 15" strip set into 10 segments 1 1/4" wide. Cut the 8" strip into five segments 1 1/4" wide.

Step 5. Combine two blue-muslin-blue segments with one muslin-blue-muslin segment to make one block as shown in Figure 3 and press; repeat for five blocks.

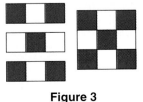

Figure 3
Join segments to make 1 block.

Project Specifications

Skill Level: Intermediate
Quilt Size: 14 1/4" x 14 1/4"
Block Size: 2 1/4" x 2 1/4"
Number of Blocks: 5

Materials

- ✔ 1/6 yard blue print
- ✔ 1/4 yard muslin
- ✔ Lightweight batting 16" x 16"
- ✔ Backing 17" x 17"
- ✔ Neutral color all-purpose thread
- ✔ Contrasting quilting thread
- ✔ 2 (5/8") plastic bone rings
- ✔ Basic sewing supplies and tools, rotary cutter, mat and ruler

Step 6. From one 2 3/4" muslin strip, cut four 2 3/4" x 2 3/4" squares.

Step 7. Arrange the pieced blocks with the muslin squares in rows as shown in Figure 4. Join the blocks in rows, pressing seams as shown in Figure 5. Join rows to complete pieced center.

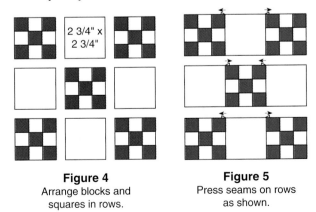

Figure 4
Arrange blocks and squares in rows.

Figure 5
Press seams on rows as shown.

Step 8. Cut one 1 1/4" blue strip into two 7 1/4" and two 8 3/4" lengths. Sew a 7 1/4" strip to opposite sides of the quilt center; press seams toward strips. Sew the 8 3/4" strips to the top and bottom; press seams toward strips. Refer to Figure 6 for strip sizes and order of

Miniature Nine-Patch
Placement Diagram
14 1/4" x 14 1/4"

Nine-Patch
2 1/4" x 2 1/4" Block

Heart Quilting Design

Border Quilting Design

sewing. *Note: All border strips may be cut longer than needed and trimmed even after stitching if desired.*

Step 9. Cut remaining 2 3/4" muslin strips into two 8 3/4" and two 13 1/4" lengths. Sew an 8 3/4" strip to opposite sides of quilt center; press seams toward strips. Sew the 13 1/4" strips to the top and bottom; press seams toward strips.

Step 10. Cut the remaining 1 1/4" blue print strips into two strips 13 1/4" long and two strips 14 3/4" long. Sew the shorter strips to opposite sides of the pieced center; press seams toward strips. Sew the longer strips to the top and bottom of the pieced center; press seams toward strips.

Step 11. Mark heart quilting designs in muslin squares and border quilting design in muslin border; prepare top for quilting referring to General Instructions.

Step 12. Quilt on marked lines and as desired by hand or machine.

Step 13. Trim batting only even with quilt top edges. Turn under backing edge 1/4"; fold remaining backing edges over to front side of quilt. Hand-stitch in place, mitering corners.

Step 14. Hand-stitch a plastic ring to each top corner on backside of quilt to finish.

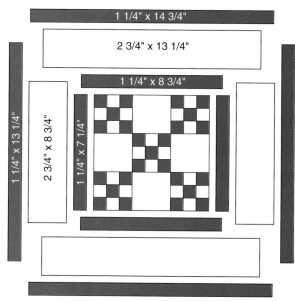

1 1/4" x 14 3/4"

2 3/4" x 13 1/4"

1 1/4" x 8 3/4"

1 1/4" x 13 1/4"

2 3/4" x 8 3/4"

1 1/4" x 7 1/4"

Figure 6
Sew border strips to pieced center as shown.

Ribbon & Stars Quilt

By Lucy A. Fazely

Hang the *Ribbon & Stars* quilt as a focal accent to any room, or add an extra row of blocks or larger borders to the top and bottom to make this quilt fit a twin-size bed.

Instructions

Note: *A 1/4" seam allowance is included in all measurements.*

Step 1. Cut the following strips 3 7/8" across the width of the fabric: 20 strips dark green; five strips each from both blue-green prints; and two each from seven light and medium prints.

Step 2. Cut four strips 5 1/2" x 63 1/2" (along length of fabric) border print. Cut one strip each from seven light and medium prints 3 1/2" by fabric width.

Step 3. From the 3 7/8" strips dark green, cut 196 squares each 3 7/8" x 3 7/8". Cut each of these squares in half on one diagonal as shown in Figure 1. ***Note:*** *Strips may be layered to cut more than one square at a time.*

Figure 1
Cut each square
on the diagonal.

Step 4. From the first medium blue-green print, cut 49 squares 3 7/8" x 3 7/8". Cut each of these squares in half on one diagonal. Sew one of these triangles to a dark green triangle to make a triangle/square as shown in

Project Specifications

Skill Level: Intermediate
Quilt Size: 73" x 73"
Block Size: 9" x 9"
Number of Blocks: 49

Materials

- ✓ 2 1/2 yards dark green print
- ✓ 2/3 yard each of 2 medium blue-green prints
- ✓ 1/2 yard each of 7 light and medium prints
- ✓ 2 yards blue-green border print
- ✓ 2 1/2 yards 90"-wide fabric for backing
- ✓ Batting 77" x 77"
- ✓ 2/3 yard dark blue print for self-made binding
- ✓ Basic sewing supplies and tools

Figure 2; press. ***Note:*** *Be careful not to stretch bias edges of triangles when stitching.* Repeat with second medium blue/green print strips.

Step 5. Cut 14 squares 3 7/8" x 3 7/8" from the 3 7/8"-wide light and medium print strips. Cut as in Step 4. Sew to dark green triangles as shown in Figure 2; press.

Step 6. Cut each of the 3 1/2" light and medium strips into seven 3 1/2" x 3 1/2" squares.

Step 7. Arrange like-colored triangle/square units in rows with blue-green units and 3 1/2" squares to create a block as shown in Figure 3. Join the units in rows; join the rows to complete one block and press. Complete 49 blocks, making seven stars from each of the seven light and medium fabrics.

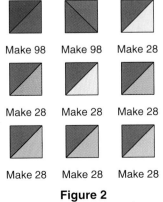

Make 98 Make 98 Make 28

Make 28 Make 28 Make 28

Make 28 Make 28 Make 28

Figure 2
Make triangle/squares as shown.

Figure 3
Arrange units to make 1 block.

Step 8. Arrange blocks in rows, positioning colors to make a diagonal pattern referring to the Placement Diagram for arrangement.

Step 9. Join the blocks in rows; press. Join rows to complete quilt center; press.

Step 10. Sew a border strip to each side of the pieced center, starting and stopping stitching at seam line as shown in Figure 4; press seams toward strips.

Step 11. Cut one square border print 8 3/8" x 8 3/8". ***Note:** The corner triangle on the quilt shown continues the matching border stripe. This requires careful planning to accomplish.* Cut the square on both diagonals to make four triangles. Set in a triangle at each corner; press. ***Note:** The straight of grain on the corner triangles will be on the outer edge to prevent stretching.*

Step 12. Prepare top for quilting and finish referring to the General Instructions section.

Ribbon & Stars
Placement Diagram
73" x 73"

Figure 4
Start and stop stitching at the seam line.

Ribbon & Stars
9" x 9" Block

Goose in the Barn

By Lucy A. Fazely

It's easy to make a bed-size quilt using this Goose in the Barn pattern. The large blocks with sashing strips between make it quick to stitch and easy to piece. Add a wide border all around and quilt a pretty design in it to show off your stitches.

Instructions

Step 1. Cut eight strips light print 2" by fabric width and seven strips dark print 2" by fabric width.

Step 2. Sew a light strip to a dark strip to a light strip. Press seams toward dark strip; repeat for three stitched strips. Cut strips into 2" segments as shown in Figure 1; you will need 48 of these segments.

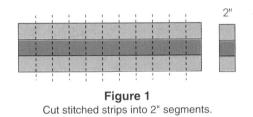

Figure 1
Cut stitched strips into 2" segments.

Step 3. Sew a dark strip to a light strip to a dark strip. Press seams toward dark strips; repeat. Cut strips into 2" segments as shown in Figure 2; you will need 24 of these segments.

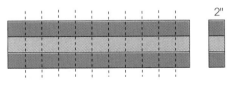

Figure 2
Cut stitched strips into 2" segments.

Figure 3
Join segments to complete
1 unit as shown.

Project Specifications

Skill Level: Beginner
Quilt Size: 61 1/2" x 87 1/2"
Block Size: 22 1/2" x 22 1/2"
Number of Blocks: 6

Materials

- ✔ 1 3/4 yards dark print
- ✔ 2 1/4 yards light print
- ✔ 2 3/4 yards dark print for sashing, borders and binding
- ✔ Backing 66" x 92"
- ✔ Batting 66" x 92"
- ✔ Neutral color all-purpose thread
- ✔ 1 spool each light and dark quilting thread
- ✔ Basic sewing supplies and tools

Step 4. Sew the segments together as shown in Figure 3 to make one Nine-Patch unit; repeat for 24 units.

Step 5. To make bar units, cut three strips light 2" by fabric width and six strips dark 2" by fabric width.

Step 6. Sew a dark strip to a light strip to a dark strip; repeat for three stitched strips. Press seams toward dark fabric.

Step 7. Cut stitched strips into 5" segments as shown in Figure 4. You will need 24 of these units.

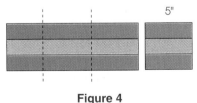

Figure 4
Join strips; cut into 5" segments.

Step 8. Cut five strips each from light and dark fabrics 5 3/8" by fabric width. Cut each strip into 5 3/8" segments to make squares. You will need 36 squares of each color.

Step 9. Cut each square in half on the diagonal to make triangles as shown in Figure 5. Sew a light triangle to a dark triangle; repeat for 72 triangles.

Figure 5
Cut squares in half on the diagonal. Stitch
together to make a triangle/square.

Step 10. Cut four strips light 5" by fabric width. Cut strips into 5" segments; repeat for 30 segments.

Step 11. Arrange triangle/squares and light squares to make one row as shown in Figure 6; join units to make a row. Repeat for 12 rows; press.

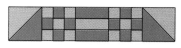

Figure 6
Make a row as shown.

Step 12. Arrange triangle/squares with Nine-Patch and bar units to make a row as shown in Figure 7; join in rows. Repeat for 12 rows; press.

Figure 7
Make a row as shown.

Step 13. Arrange light squares with bar units to make a row as shown in Figure 8; join in rows. Repeat for six rows; press.

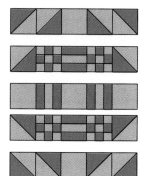

Figure 8
Make a row as shown.

Step 14. Arrange the rows pieced in Steps 11, 12 and 13 to make one block as shown in Figure 9; join the rows. Repeat for six blocks; press.

Step 15. Cut a 22" x 44" rectangle; set aside to make self-made binding referring to General Instructions.

Step 16. Cut three strips of border fabric 4" x 23". Join two blocks with a strip as shown in Figure 10; repeat for three rows. Press seams toward strips.

Step 17. Cut two strips border fabric 4" x 49". Join the rows with these strips as shown in Figure 10. Press seams toward strips.

Step 18. Cut two 7" x 75" strips border fabric. Sew to

opposite long sides of pieced center; press seams toward strips. Cut two 7" x 62" strips; sew a strip to the top and bottom of pieced center. Press seams toward strips.

Step 19. Mark quilting design given in the borders. *Note: The quilt shown is hand-quilted in the ditch of the blocks and sashing strips and on the borders using the design given.*

Step 20. Prepare top for quilting and finish referring to General Instructions.

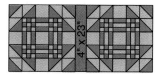

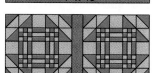

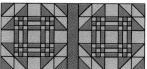

Figure 9
Join rows to make 1 block as shown.

Figure 10
Join blocks and rows with
sashing strips as shown.

Border Quilting Design

Connect here

Goose in the Barn
22 1/2" x 22 1/2" Block

Goose in the Barn
Placement Diagram
61 1/2" x 87 1/2"

6 1/2" x 74 1/2"

6 1/2" x 61 1/2"

Connect here

Twist & Turn Nine-Patch

By Holly Daniels

Can you see the Nine-Patch within a Nine-Patch in this quilt? The pretty gold colors combine with muslin and navy to create a neat optical illusion. All that teamed up with quick methods, and you have a winner.

Instructions

Step 1. Cut A pieces using template given. Cut the following strips across the width of the fabric: nine 3" gold-on-gold print; and four 3" gold-and-blue floral.

Step 2. Sew strips cut in Step 1 to make two gold-floral-gold and one floral-gold-floral strip sets as shown in Figure 1; press seams toward gold.

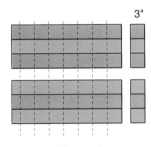

Figure 1
Make strip sets as shown;
cut into 3" segments.

Step 3. Cut strip sets into 3" segments as shown in Figure 1. Sew segments together to form a Nine-Patch unit as shown in Figure 2; press seams to one side. Repeat for nine Nine-Patch units.

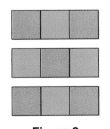

Figure 2
Join segments to make
Nine-Patch block.

Step 4. Sew a muslin A and a navy A together to make a rectangle as shown in Figure 3; press seams toward dark fabric; repeat for 36 units.

Project Specifications

Skill Level: Beginner
Quilt Size: 44" x 44"
Block Size: 12 1/2" x 12 1/2"
Number of Blocks: 9

Materials

- ✔ 3/4 yard gold-and-blue floral print
- ✔ 3/4 yard gold-on-gold print
- ✔ 3/4 yard muslin
- ✔ 1 yard navy-on-navy print
- ✔ Backing 48" x 48"
- ✔ Batting 48" x 48"
- ✔ Neutral color all-purpose thread
- ✔ 5 yards self-made or purchased binding
- ✔ Basic sewing supplies and tools, rotary cutter, ruler and cutting mat

Figure 3
Sew A to A.

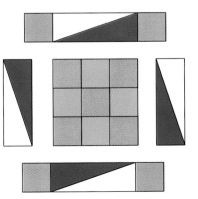

Figure 4
Join units to complete 1 block.

93

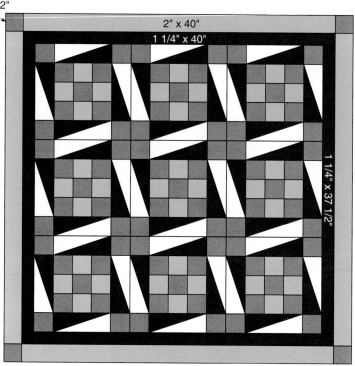

Twist & Turn
12 1/2" x 12 1/2" Block

2" x 2"

2" x 40"
1 1/4" x 40"

1 1/4" x 37 1/2"

Twist & Turn Nine-Patch
Placement Diagram
44" x 44"

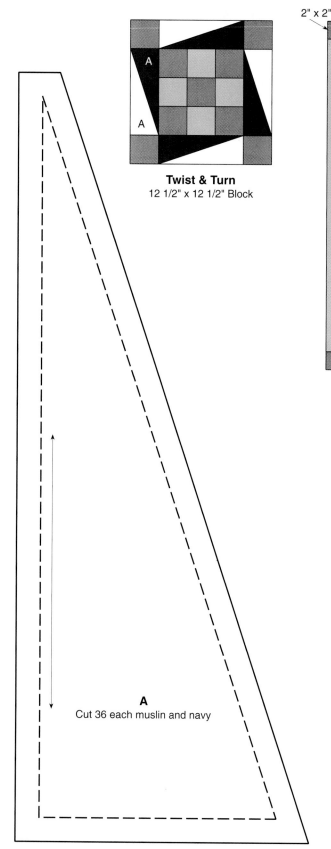

A
Cut 36 each muslin and navy

Step 5. Cut the remaining gold-on-gold strips into 3" segments. Sew one of these segments to each end of 18 of the A-A rectangles; press.

Step 6. Sew an A-A rectangle to opposite sides of a pieced Nine-Patch unit. Sew two A-A with gold square units to the remaining sides to complete one block referring to Figure 4; press and repeat for nine blocks.

Step 7. Arrange blocks in three rows of three blocks each. Join in rows; press. Join rows; press.

Step 8. Cut two strips navy-on-navy print 1 3/4" x 38". Sew a strip to opposite sides of pieced center; press seams toward strips. Cut two more strips 1 3/4" x 40 1/2". Sew a strip to the top and bottom; press seams toward strips.

Step 9. Cut four strips gold-and-blue floral 2 1/2" x 40 1/2". Sew a strip to two opposite sides of the pieced center; press seams toward strips. Cut four squares gold print 2 1/2" x 2 1/2"; sew one of these squares to each end of the two remaining strips. Sew a strip to the top and bottom; press seams toward strips.

Step 10. Prepare top for quilting and finish referring to General Instructions.

Forever Spring

By Joyce Livingston

Spring! New life, new beginnings. The promise of good things to come. A time of refreshing, a bursting forth of color. Make this Nine-Patch quilt from beautiful, bright colors and add your favorite flower appliqués, and you'll have spring on your wall anytime you want it.

Project Notes

Use a piece of foam insulation board covered with an old white sheet to pin the Nine-Patch blocks to as they are completed. This allows you to arrange and rearrange them to create a pleasing pattern before sewing them together.

Use a see-through plastic 6" x 6" ruler to square up the completed Nine-Patch blocks.

Allow your floral appliquéd flowers to drift over into the border for added eye appeal. Use a 1/4" seam allowance for all seams. If you decide to machine-quilt, you may prefer to quilt the center of the top before adding the border to eliminate knotting at the beginning and ending of your stitching.

Instructions

Step 1. Cut a varying number of strips from each of the 14 colors 2" across fabric width. Divide the colors into seven light/dark complementary pairs.

Step 2. Stitch a dark, light and dark strip together along length; press seam to dark side. Stitch a light, dark and light strip together along length; press seam to dark side.

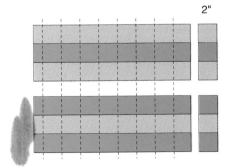

Figure 1
Sew 2 sets of strips using lights and darks as shown.

Project Specifications

Skill Level: Intermediate
Quilt Size: 42" x 46 1/2"
Block Size: 4 1/2" x 4 1/2"
Number of Blocks: 68

Materials

- 1 yard colorful floral print
- 1/2 yard each of 7 light and 7 dark fabrics
- 1 1/2 yards dark solid for borders and binding
- Backing 46" x 50"
- Batting 46" x 50"
- Neutral color all-purpose thread
- 1 spool contrasting quilting thread
- 1 spool clear monofilament thread
- 1 1/2 yards fusible transfer web
- Basic sewing supplies and tools and 6" x 6" see-through ruler

Step 3. Cut strips into 2" segments as shown in Figure 1.

Step 4. Join segments to create 68 Nine-Patch units as shown in Figure 2. Press and square blocks to 5" x 5".

Figure 2
Join strip sets to make Nine-Patch blocks.

Step 5. Cut four squares 5" x 5" from floral print.

Step 6. Arrange the Nine-Patch units and the four floral squares in nine rows of eight blocks each. ***Note:*** *Rearrange blocks to make a pleasing arrangement or refer to the quilt shown for suggestions.*

Step 7. Join blocks in rows; press. Join rows to complete pieced center.

Step 8. Cut two border strips 3 1/2" x 36 1/2" along length of border fabric. Sew a strip to the top and

Nine-Patch
4 1/2" x 4 1/2" Block

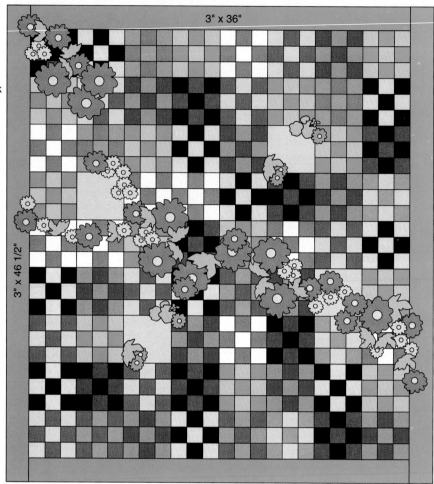

Forever Spring
Placement Diagram
42" x 46 1/2"

bottom of the pieced center; press seams toward strips. Cut two border strips 3 1/2" x 47" along length of border fabric. Sew a strip to opposite sides of the quilt center; press seams toward strips.

Step 9. Fuse transfer web to the wrong side of the floral print following manufacturer's instructions; remove paper backing. Using small, sharp-tipped scissors, cut flower and leaf groups from fused floral print.

Step 10. Place the cutout flowers on the pieced top in a pleasing arrangement. Fuse in place following manufacturer's instructions.

Step 11. Machine-appliqué around shapes using a machine blanket stitch or medium-width satin stitch and monofilament or contrasting thread in the top of the machine and neutral color all-purpose thread in the bobbin.

Step 12. Prepare top for quilting and finish referring to General Instructions.

Pig in a Nine-Patch

By Ann Boyce

If you are a pig collector, you also like to make quilted projects using your porky friend. Try making this simple wall quilt to let the world know that, in your home, pigs are welcome.

Instructions

Step 1. Cut 13 squares blue star print 8" x 8".

Step 2. Cut 12 squares 3" x 3" from each of the nine 1/8-yard fabric pieces.

Step 3. Sew a pink square to a beige square to a green square; repeat for 12 units. Sew a beige square to a blue square to a beige square; repeat for 12 units. Sew a green square to a beige square to a purple square; repeat for 12 units.

Step 4. Join the pieced units as shown in Figure 1 to complete one Nine-Patch block; repeat for 12 blocks.

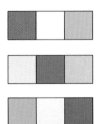

Figure 1
Make Nine-Patch
block as shown.

Step 5. Prepare templates for star, pig and bow pieces using pattern pieces given. Reverse patterns and trace 13 stars, 13 pigs and 13 bows onto the paper side of the fusible transfer web. Fuse the star drawings to the wrong side of the yellow print, the pig drawings to the wrong side of the pink print and the bow drawings to

Figure 2
Fuse pig to star as shown.

Project Specifications

Skill Level: Beginner
Project Size: 41 1/2" x 41 1/2"
Block Size: 7 1/2" x 7 1/2"
Number of Blocks: 12 Nine-Patch and 13 Pig blocks

Materials

- 1/8 yard each 4 different beige prints, 2 different green prints
- 1/8 yard each blue, purple and pink prints
- 1/3 yard beige print for borders
- 3/4 yard blue star print
- 2/3 yard yellow print
- 1/4 yard pink print
- 1/8 yard green plaid
- Backing 45" x 45"
- Batting 45" x 45"
- 5 yards self-made or purchased pink binding
- 2 spools each yellow and pink and 1 spool green and neutral color all-purpose thread
- 1 spool clear nylon monofilament
- 3 yards fusible transfer web
- 1 1/2 yards tear-off fabric stabilizer
- 13 (1/4") blue buttons
- Basic sewing supplies and tools

the wrong side of the green plaid following manufacturer's instructions. Cut out shapes; remove paper backing.

Step 6. Fuse star to center of a blue-star square. Fuse pig in the center of the star as shown in Figure 2 referring to dotted lines on star pattern for placement. Fuse bow to pig referring to dotted lines on pig for placement. Repeat for 13 blocks.

Step 7. Cut 13 squares 8" x 8" from fabric stabilizer. Pin a square to the backside of each fused block.

Step 8. Using a machine zigzag stitch and thread to match shapes, appliqué stars, pigs and bows in place.

Step 9. Sew a button to each pig shape using the X on the pattern as a guide for placement.

Step 10. Join three appliquéd blocks with two Nine-Patch blocks to make a row as shown in Figure 3; repeat for three rows.

Figure 3
Join blocks to make a row as shown.

Step 11. Join three Nine-Patch blocks with two appliquéd blocks to make a row as shown in Figure 4; repeat for two rows.

Step 12. Join the rows referring to the Placement Diagram; press.

Step 13. Cut two strips beige print 2 1/2" x 38"; sew a strip to opposite sides of quilt center. Press seams toward strips. Cut two more

strips 2 1/2" x 42"; sew a strip to the top and bottom. Press seams toward strips.

Step 14. Prepare top for quilting and finish referring to General Instructions. ***Note:** The quilt shown was machine-quilted using monofilament thread in the top of the machine and neutral color all-purpose thread in the bobbin. Quilting was done in the ditch of the*

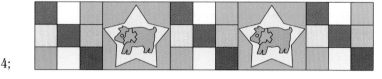

Figure 4
Join blocks to make a row as shown.

borders and blocks, from corner to corner in the Nine-Patch blocks and 1/8" from edge of star shapes in the appliquéd blocks.

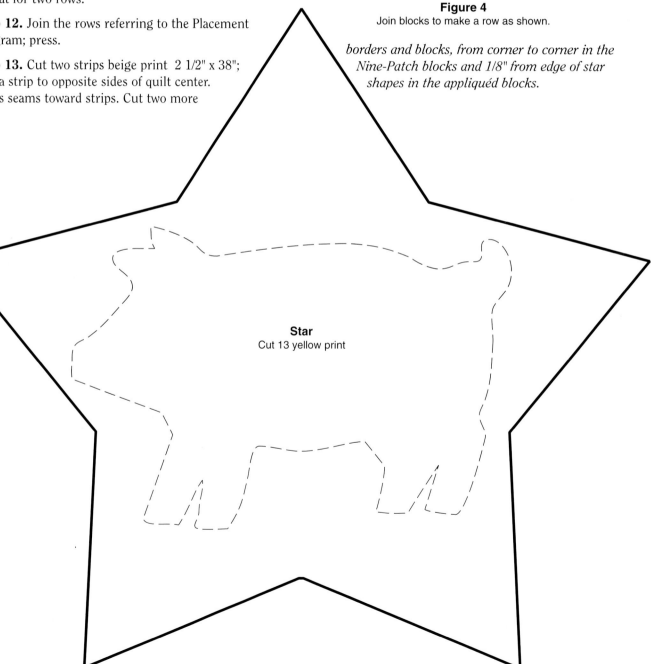

Star
Cut 13 yellow print

Nine-Patch
7 1/2" x 7 1/2" Block

Pig in a Star
7 1/2" x 7 1/2" Block

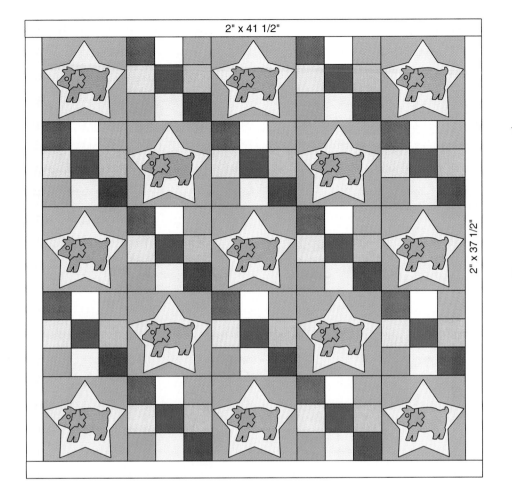

Pig in a Nine-Patch
Placement Diagram
41 1/2" x 42 1/2"

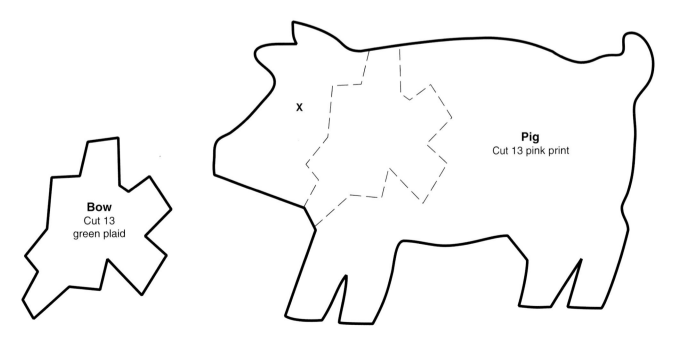

Bow
Cut 13
green plaid

X

Pig
Cut 13 pink print

101

True Lover's Knot

By Sandra L. Hatch

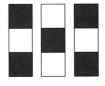

This quilt was made to duplicate an antique blue-and-white quilt from the late 1800s. Today the way the blocks are put together and the border treatment on that quilt would be changed. An alternative design would be to have smaller blocks in each border corner and navy blue sashing squares with the solid white sashing strips between blocks. If these changes are appealing to you, see Figure 1 for placement.

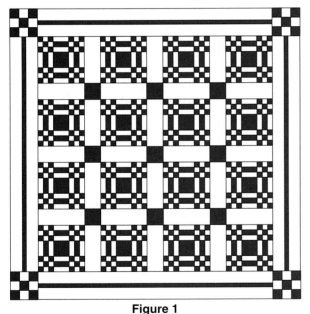

Figure 1
A better design is formed when dark sashing squares or Nine-Patch blocks are placed at the block corners in the sashing. Border corners would also look better with a block in the corner.

Instructions

Step 1. Cut 25 strips navy blue print and 29 strips white solid 2" by fabric width.

Step 2. Sew a white strip to a navy strip to a white strip; press seams toward the navy strip. Repeat for 11 strip sets. Cut three strip sets into 2" segments and eight strip sets into 5" segments referring to Figure 2.

Project Specifications

Skill Level: Beginner
Quilt Size: 78" x 78"
Block Size: 13 1/2" x 13 1/2"
Number of Blocks: 16

Materials

- 4 1/4 yards navy blue print
- 4 1/2 yards white solid
- Backing 82" x 82"
- Batting 82" x 82"
- 2 spools white all-purpose thread
- 1 spool navy quilting thread
- Basic sewing supplies and tools
- 8 3/4 yards self-made or purchased binding

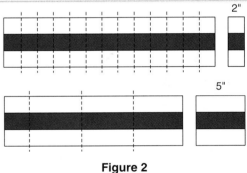

Figure 2
Cut white/blue/white strip sets
in 2" and 5" segments.

Step 3. Sew a navy strip to a white strip to a navy strip; press seams toward the navy strips. Repeat for seven strip sets. Cut each strip into 2" segments.

Step 4. Sew a white/navy/white segment between two navy/white/navy segments to complete one Nine-Patch unit as shown in Figure 3. Repeat for 64 units.

Figure 3
Make Nine-Patch
blocks as shown.

1 1/2" x 78"

2 1/4" x 78"

1 1/2" x 66"

True Lover's Knot
Placement Diagram
13 1/2" x 13 1/2"

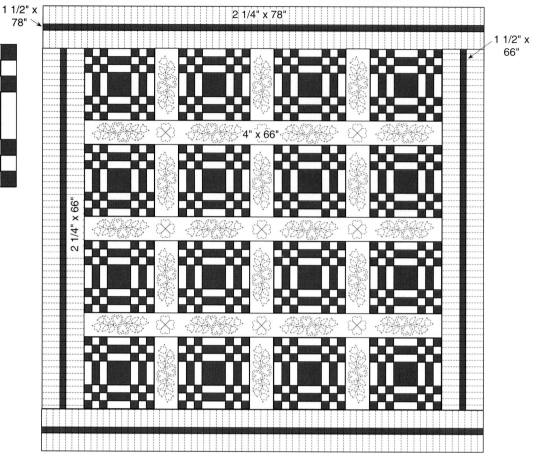

4" x 66"

2 1/4" x 66"

True Lover's Knot
Placement Diagram
78" x 78"

Step 5. Cut two strips 5" by fabric width navy blue print. Cut strips into 5" segments. You will need 16 segments.

Step 6. Arrange the stitched units in rows with a 5" segment as shown in Figure 4. Join units in rows; join rows to complete one block. Press; repeat for 16 blocks.

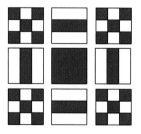

Figure 4
Arrange stitched units in
rows to make 1 block.

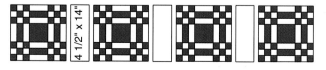

4 1/2" x 14"

Figure 5
Join 4 blocks with 3 strips.

Step 7. Cut 12 strips white 4 1/2" x 14". Join four blocks with three strips to make one row as shown in Figure 5; press seams toward strips. Repeat for four rows.

Step 8. Cut three strips 4 1/2" x 66 1/2" white solid. Join the block rows with these strips to complete pieced center.

Step 9. Cut two strips navy 2" x 66 1/2" and four strips white 2 3/4" x 66 1/2". Sew a navy strip between two white strips; press seams toward navy. Repeat for a second strip. Sew a pieced strip to opposite sides of the quilt center.

Step 10. Cut two strips navy 2" x 78 1/2" and four strips white 2 3/4" x 78 1/2". Sew as in Step 9 and sew to top and bottom; press seams toward strips.

Step 11. Mark sashing strips with quilting designs given referring to the Placement Diagram for arrangement. Mark border strips with straight lines perpendicular to the quilt center for quilting.

Step 12. Prepare top for quilting and finish referring to General Instructions.

True Lover's Knot

**Sashing
Quilting
Design**

Sashing Quilting Design

Seeing Spots

By Lucy A. Fazely

Novelty prints can be the inspiration for a quilt. The spotted print used in this quilt combines with a neat dog print with Spot doing his favorite things. It is hard to see the Nine-Patch in the design, but it is there if you look.

Instructions

Step 1. From novelty print cut one square 12 1/2" x 12 1/2" and four strips 6 1/2" by remaining fabric width. Cut strips into 6 1/2" segments. You will need 20 segments.

Step 2. Cut three strips red print 3 1/2" by fabric width and nine strips white print 3 1/2" by fabric width.

Step 3. Sew a red print strip to a white print strip; press seams toward the red print strip; repeat for three strip sets. Cut 12 segments from each strip 3 1/2" wide as shown in Figure 1.

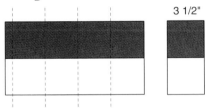

Figure 1
Cut stitched strips into 3 1/2" segments.

Step 4. Cut the remaining white print strips into 6 1/2" segments; you will need 36 of these 3 1/2" x 6 1/2" segments.

Step 5. Sew a 3 1/2" x 6 1/2" white print segment to one segment cut in Step 3 as shown in Figure 2.

3 1/2" x 6 1/2"

3 1/2" x 3 1/2"

Figure 2
Join 2 segments as shown.

Step 6. Cut the following strips across fabric width for Nine-Patch blocks: five blue print 2 1/2" wide; four white print 2 1/2" wide; and three white print 4 1/2" wide.

Project Specifications

Skill Level: Beginner
Quilt Size: 54" x 66"
Block Size: 6" x 6"
Number of Blocks: 20 Nine-Patch and 36 Four-Patch

Materials

- ✔ 3/4 yard novelty print
- ✔ 1/3 yard red print
- ✔ 1 3/4 yards white print (white with black spots on quilt)
- ✔ 1 1/2 yards blue print (for blocks, borders and self-made binding)
- ✔ Backing 58" x 70"
- ✔ Batting 58" x 70"
- ✔ Neutral color all-purpose thread
- ✔ Basic sewing supplies and tools

Step 7. Sew a 2 1/2"-wide white strip to a 2 1/2"-wide blue strip to a 2 1/2"-wide white strip; repeat. Press seams toward the blue strip. Cut stitched strips into 2 1/2" segments as shown in Figure 3.

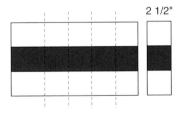

Figure 3
Join strips; cut into 2 1/2" segments.

Step 8. Sew a 2 1/2"-wide blue strip to a 4 1/2" white strip; repeat for three stitched strips. Press seams toward the blue strip. Cut strips into 2 1/2" segments as shown in Figure 4.

Step 9. Join a segment cut in Step 7 with two segments cut in Step 8 to make a Nine-Patch block as shown in Figure 5; repeat for 20 blocks. ***Note:*** *To avoid making reversed sections, the pieced units are turned in all different directions to make the design. Individual pieces*

2 1/2"

Figure 4
Join strips; cut into 2 1/2" segments.

Figure 5
Join segments to make
a Nine-Patch block.

6 1/2" x
6 1/2"

12 1/2" x
12 1/2"

Figure 6
Arrange Four-Patch blocks with
Nine-Patch blocks, 6 1/2" squares
and 12 1/2" square as shown.

3" x 54"

3" x 60"

Seeing Spots
Placement Diagram
54" x 66"

in each unit may not be placed in exactly the same
position as the pieces in the unit next to it. Follow the
Placement Diagram and Figure 6 carefully to avoid
confusion.

Step 10. Arrange Four-Patch blocks with Nine-Patch
blocks and the 12 1/2" x 12 1/2" and 6 1/2" x 6 1/2"
squares cut in Step 1 to make rows as shown in

Figure 6. Join the blocks in rows; press. Join rows and
press to complete pieced center.

Step 11. Prepare two strips blue print 3 1/2" x 60 1/2".
*Note: With yardage given, strips are cut across fabric
width and joined on short ends to make strips long
enough for borders. If you prefer unpieced strips, more
blue fabric would be needed than given in the list of
materials.* Sew a strip to opposite long sides of the quilt
center. Press seams toward strips.

Step 12. Cut two strips blue print 3 1/2" x 54 1/2";
sew to top and bottom of pieced center. Press seams
toward strips.

Step 13. Prepare top for quilting and finish referring to
General Instructions.

108

I Heard It Through the Grapevine

By Sandra L. Hatch

The fabric line chosen to make this quilt inspired the name. The different shades of purple combine with the green to create a contemporary quilt.

Project Notes

Similar to the Log Cabin, the block used to create this quilt combines with other blocks in many different ways to create a totally different quilt. Figure 13 on page 119 shows three different variations, depending on how the blocks are placed in each row.

You may choose to lay your blocks out to make even a different version. The fun part is playing with the blocks before sewing them together. If you have a computer with a drawing program, this part is easier, but drawings don't show the fabrics as they really are. You may still want to lay the blocks out in a variety of positions before choosing your favorite.

If you have an instant camera, it would help to photograph the blocks in each layout before picking them up and trying a different one. After you are done playing it is easy to then view each layout in the photos and choose the one you like the best.

Instructions

Step 1. Cut six strips 3 1/2" by fabric width each tan-on-tan, medium purple and purple-on-purple prints.

Step 2. Cut 12 strips each 3 1/2" by fabric width green and dark purple prints.

Step 3. Cut seven strips each 3 7/8" by fabric width green and dark purple prints.

Figure 1
Sew a dark purple, medium purple and green print strip together; cut into 3 1/2" segments.

Step 4. Sew a 3 1/2" dark purple print strip to a 3 1/2" medium purple strip to a 3 1/2" green strip. Press

Project Specifications

Skill Level: Intermediate
Quilt Size: 96" x 96"
Block Size: 9" x 9"
Number of Blocks: 64

Materials

- 1 yard each tan-on-tan, medium purple and purple-on-purple prints
- 2 1/2 yards each green and dark purple prints
- Fat quarter each 3 coordinating prints
- 1/2 yard green/purple/beige print
- 2 3/4 yards coordinating print for borders
- Backing 100" x 100"
- Batting 100" x 100"
- 3 spools neutral color all-purpose thread
- Quilting thread
- 12 1/4 yards self-made or purchased binding
- Basic sewing supplies and tools

seams toward green strip. Repeat for six strip units. Cut each strip into twelve 3 1/2" segments as shown in Figure 1 to make center row of blocks. You will need 64 segments. Set aside any extras.

Step 5. Sew a 3 1/2" tan-on-tan strip to a 3 1/2" green strip. Press seams toward green strip. Repeat for six strip units. Cut twelve 3 1/2" segments from each strip as shown in Figure 2. Repeat with 3 1/2" purple-on-purple strips and dark purple print strips.

Figure 2
Sew a tan-on-tan strip to a green print strip; cut into 3 1/2" segments.

Step 6. Lay a 3 7/8" green strip on a 3 7/8" dark purple print strip right sides together. Align perfectly. ***Note:*** *It might help to press the strips together using an iron.* Cut 3 7/8" segments from pressed strips. Cut segments in half

109

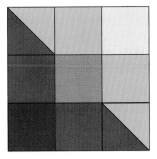

Grapevine
9" x 9" Block

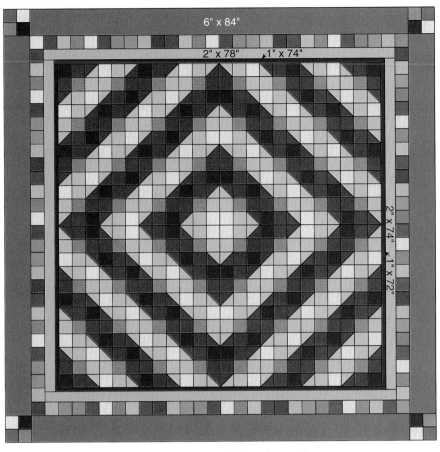

I Heard It Through the Grapevine
Placement Diagram
96" x 96"

on one diagonal to make triangles as shown in Figure 3. *Note: The cut triangles are layered and ready to sew.*

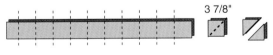

Figure 3
Lay a green print strip on a dark purple print strip; cut into 3 7/8" segments.

Step 7. Sew across the cut diagonal to make triangle/squares as shown in Figure 4. Repeat with all 3 7/8" strips. You will need 128 triangle/squares.

Figure 4
Sew across diagonal of cut squares to make triangle/squares.

Figure 5
Sew a triangle/square to a pieced tan and green segment.

Step 8. Sew a triangle/square to the pieced tan-on-tan and green segments as shown in Figure 5; repeat for 64 units. Press seams toward the triangle/square unit.

Step 9. Sew a triangle/square to the pieced purple-on-purple and dark purple print segments as shown in Figure 6; repeat for 64 units. Press seams toward purple print squares. *Note: It is easy to get the triangles turned and stitched in the wrong direction. Carefully check first unit against the figure drawings to be sure you are stitching all units correctly.*

Step 10. Sew a unit stitched in Step 8 to a unit stitched in Step 4 as shown in Figure 7; repeat for 64 units. Press seams toward center.

Figure 6
Sew a triangle/square to a pieced purple-on-purple and dark purple print segment.

Figure 7
Join segments as shown.

Step 11. Sew a unit stitched in Step 9 to the bottom of a unit stitched in Step 10 as shown in Figure 8; repeat for 64 units. Press seams toward center to complete the blocks.

111

Step 12. Lay out blocks in eight rows of eight blocks each referring to Figure 9. *Note: Be careful to pin rows in the exact order and number rows to avoid confusion when sewing rows together.* Join blocks in rows; press. Join the rows; press to complete pieced center.

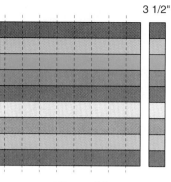

3 1/2"

Figure 10
Cut stitched strip unit into 3 1/2" segments.

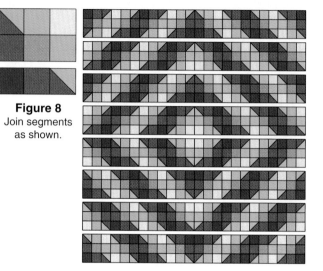

Figure 8
Join segments as shown.

Figure 9
Lay blocks out in rows.

Step 13. Cut two strips purple-on-purple print 1 1/2" x 72 1/2". Sew to opposite sides of quilt center; press seams toward strips. Cut two more strips 1 1/2" x 74 1/2". Sew to top and bottom; press seams toward strips.

Step 14. Cut two strips green/purple/beige print 2 1/2" x 74 1/2". Sew to opposite sides of quilt center; press seams toward strips. Cut two more strips 2 1/2" x 78 1/2". Sew to top and bottom; press seams toward strips.

Step 15. Cut one strip 3 1/2" by fabric width from each fabric except border print (nine fabrics total). Join the strips in any order along length. Press seams in one direction.

Step 16. Cut stitched strip unit into 3 1/2" segments as shown in Figure 10. Join three segments four times as shown in Figure 11. Sew a stitched strip to opposite sides, removing one square from one end of each strip before stitching; press seams toward previously stitched border strip.

Figure 11
Join 3 strip segments.

Step 17. Add one square to one end of the remaining two stitched strips. Sew one of these strips to the top and bottom of the pieced center, pressing as before.

Step 18. Make a Four-Patch block referring to Figure 12 and using four leftover squares. Repeat for four blocks.

Step 19. Cut four strips border print 6 1/2" x 84 1/2". Sew a strip to two opposite sides of the pieced center; press seams toward strips. Sew a Four-Patch block to each end of the remaining two strips. Sew these strips to the top and bottom of the pieced center; press seams toward strips.

Figure 12
Make a Four-Patch block as shown.

Step 20. Prepare top for quilting and finish referring to General Instructions.

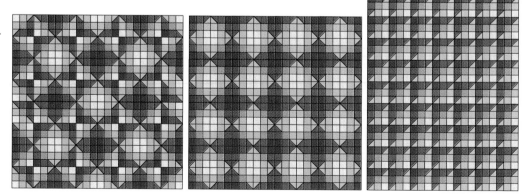

Figure 13
The above drawings show alternate arrangements for blocks.

Milky Way Crib Quilt

By Xenia Cord

Four-Patch corner blocks combine with triangle/squares to create this simple Nine-Patch crib quilt. Choose colors for either a girl or boy or a combination of both to make your own version for the little one in your life.

Instructions

Step 1. Cut eight strips each white and pink pin dot 2" by fabric width.

Step 2. Sew a pink strip to a white strip four times. Press seams toward pink strip. Cut strips into 2" segments. Join two segments to make Four-Patch units as shown in Figure 1; repeat for 39 units.

Figure 1
Join 2 segments to make
Four-Patch units.

Step 3. Cut three strips each pink floral and green print 3 7/8" by fabric width. Layer a pink strip on a green strip right sides together, keeping edges aligned. Cut each layered strip into 3 7/8" segments. Cut each segment across one diagonal to make two triangles from each layered segment.

Step 4. Stitch along diagonal; open and press seams to green side to reveal pink/green triangle/squares as shown in Figure 2. Repeat for 58 units.

Figure 2
Make 58 triangle/squares.

Step 5. Cut one strip green print 3 1/2" by fabric width. Cut strip into 3 1/2" segments. You will need 12 of these squares. Repeat with one pink floral strip.

Step 6. Join five Four-Patch units with four triangle/square units to make a Four-Patch row, making noted number of both versions as shown in Figure 3; press. *Note: Units may be stitched to make blocks as shown in Figure 4. If using this method, several different*

Project Specifications

Skill Level: Beginner
Quilt Size: 43" x 55"

Materials

- ✔ 1/2 yard each off-white solid, dark pink pin dot and green print
- ✔ 2 yards pink floral print
- ✔ Backing 47" x 59"
- ✔ Batting 47" x 59"
- ✔ Off-white all-purpose thread
- ✔ 6 yards self-made or purchased binding
- ✔ Basic sewing supplies and tools

pieced units must be made to complete quilt as shown. It is much simpler to piece units in rows. Other layout variations may be desired for which piecing blocks would be a better choice.

Make 3

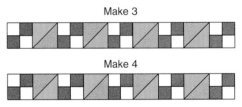

Make 4

Figure 3
Make Four-Patch rows as shown.

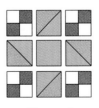

Figure 4
Join units to make 1 block as shown.

Step 7. Join five triangle/square units with two green print and two pink floral print 3 1/2" squares to make a square row as shown in Figure 5; repeat for six rows.

Step 8. Alternating Four-Patch rows with square rows referring to Figure 6, join rows to complete pieced center.

113

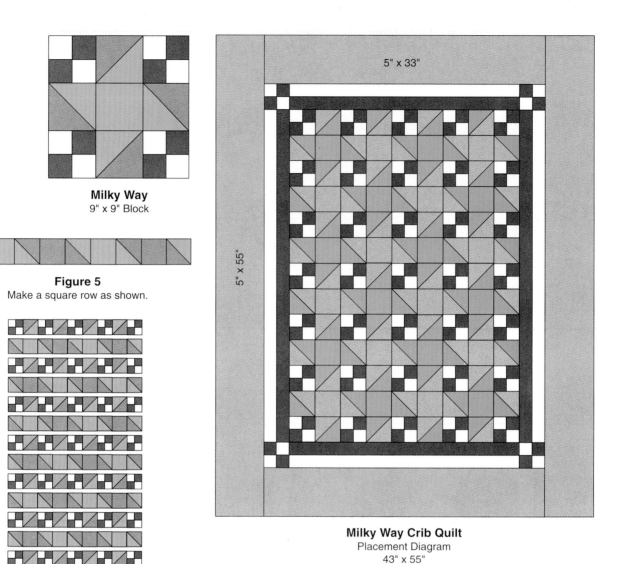

Milky Way
9" x 9" Block

Figure 5
Make a square row as shown.

Figure 6
Alternate Four-Patch rows with square rows
to complete pieced center.

Milky Way Crib Quilt
Placement Diagram
43" x 55"

Step 9. Using strips cut in Step 1, cut two strips each white and pink pin dot 2" x 27 1/2". Sew a white strip to a pink strip; repeat. Press seams toward pink. Sew to top and bottom of pieced center; press seams toward strips.

Step 10. Using strips cut in Step 1, cut two strips each white and pink pin dot 2" x 39 1/2". Sew a white strip to a pink strip; repeat. Press seams toward pink. Sew a Four-Patch unit to each end of each strip. Sew a strip to

each opposite long side of the pieced center; press seams toward strips.

Step 11. Cut two strips pink floral print 5 1/2" x 33 1/2"; sew to top and bottom. Cut two more strips 5 1/2" x 55 1/2". Sew to opposite long sides; press seams toward strips.

Step 12. Prepare top for quilting and finish referring to General Instructions.

Contemporary Nine-Patch

*C*reate a more contemporary look using Nine-Patch blocks and the patterns included in this section. Whether you want a bed quilt, a wall quilt, a wearable or an accessory, the versatile Nine-Patch pattern can be used in creative ways to make almost anything.

The use of black fabric in this striking quilt complements the brilliance of the hand-dyed rainbow fabric. When making this quilt, be ready to experiment and have fun.

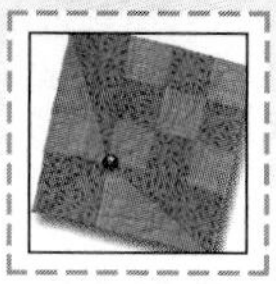

Nouveau Nine-Patch

By Melody Johnson

Who doesn't love a Nine-Patch? It may have been your first hand-cut and hand-sewn quilt block or the one consistently chosen as the basis for the many baby quilts for expectant relatives and friends. Nine-Patches are a first thought when making use of scraps, as it is possible to use nine different fabrics in one block and still maintain the classic look.

Nine-Patch quilts are simple and direct and offer an endless variety of settings. A Nine-Patch of Nine-Patches is a personal favorite, using a theme fabric as the alternating block. And a Nine-Patch border works itself into so many traditional and unconventional quilts because of its clean design and size variability.

One of my favorite qualities of this block is its frugality. Nothing is wasted in its construction. Seams are easy to match, assembly is a snap, and size can be teeny to tremendous. One can cut and sew strips which can then be cut into sections and reassembled into a Nine-Patch, resulting in an assembly line for quick quilting. What a great way to spend a few moments at the machine! In a few short hours stacks of patches can grow into wonderful quilts.

For my quilt *Nouveau Nine-Patch,* I decided to use just two fabrics: a black cotton and a 3-yard length of my hand-dyed Spectrum Stripes, which runs in a striped rainbow from selvage to selvage. My approach was to make multiple blocks with the hand-dyed fabric in four sizes: 3", 6", 9" and 12". Then I used the black cotton to set off the color and to make the connector strips that separate the blocks.

I made many more blocks than I needed for one quilt and used the leftovers for a second quilt. I like the second one even better than the first! I also intended to find a way to update this classic and chose the new look of curved seaming. This is easier than it looks, as no templates are used, and two blocks are cut at once. They are duplicates and can be sewn as mirror images if the fabric is flipped.

Risk takers may want to give this a try, while the timid

Project Specifications

Skill Level: Beginner
Project Size: Varies
Block Size: Varies
Number of Blocks: Varies

Materials

✔ 3 yards theme fabric—rainbow-hued hand-dyed or printed fabric
✔ 1 1/2 yards black cotton
✔ Backing 2" larger than quilt top all around
✔ Batting 2" larger than quilt top all around
✔ All-purpose thread to match fabrics
✔ 1 spool transparent monofilament thread
✔ Basic sewing supplies and tools

might want to practice on scrap fabric first. One helpful note: Remember to cut the fabric with right sides up at all times. And when sewing the curved patches together, the blocks may become slightly askew. This is expected and is not a mistake. Curved seams are built into this design, and give it a less rigid, more playful look. Be ready to experiment and have fun!

Nine-Patch Blocks

Step 1. Cut two strips each 3", 6", 9" and 12" across fabric width from theme fabric. Cut squares from each strip; for example, cut 3"-wide strips into 3" segments to make 3" x 3" squares. ***Note:** Because the fabric changes color from one edge to the other, each of the squares will be colored differently as shown in Figure 1.*

Figure 1
Squares cut from theme fabric will be different colors.

Step 2. Choose two squares that contrast such as yellow and purple. Lay the two contrasting squares right side up on top of each other, lining up the sides perfectly as shown in Figure 2.

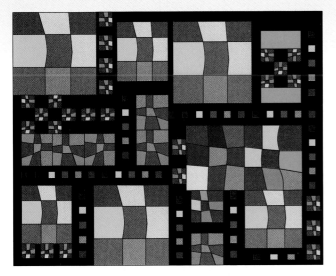

Nouveau Nine-Patch
Placement Diagram
Approximately 32" x 41 1/2"

Figure 2
Lay 1 square on top of another
wrong side against right side.
Note that the drawing shows
pieces not layered exactly.

Step 3. Using a sharp rotary cutter, cut two vertical cuts and two horizontal cuts as shown in Figure 3. *Note: The cut lines need not be parallel or straight. Do not use a straight edge for these cuts as the desired effect is a gentle curving seam line.*

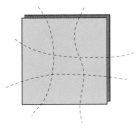

Figure 3
Make 2 horizontal and 2 vertical
cuts through both squares.

Step 4. Separate the two layers of fabric; reassemble into two blocks with contrasting patches as shown in Figure 4. Seam allowances are not a consideration in this method. Using a scant 1/4" seam, the sections will be eased together and will fit. Make curving Nine-Patch

blocks from all the squares cut from each strip, in each of the four sizes. ***Note:*** *Figure 5 shows blocks similar to those used in the sample quilt. It is not possible to copy the sample exactly. You are encouraged to use the method to create your own one-of-a-kind quilt.*

Figure 4
Reassemble pieces to make
Nine-Patch blocks with
uneven-size pieces.

Figure 5
Various blocks can be made
using this uneven cutting method
and different size squares.

Connector Strips

Step 1. From the theme fabric, cut strips 1 1/2" across fabric width and pair with 1 1/2" by fabric width strips of black cotton. Sew one of each together and join with alternating colored sets of strips as shown in Figure 6. Cut strips into 1 1/2" segments.

1 1/2"

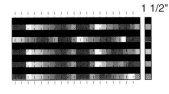

Figure 6
Sew theme fabric strips with
black strips; join stitched strips
and cut into 1 1/2" segments.

Step 2. Combine the pieced segments with 1 1/2" strips of black cotton to form setting, or connector, strips as shown in Figure 7. ***Note:*** *These strips may be joined*

Figure 7
Join pieced segments with
black connector strips.

Continued on page 127

Funky Fish Lap Quilt

By Holly Daniels

Nine-Patch blocks make up the bodies of these bright-colored tropical fish. Choose fabrics similar to those used here or select bright-colored fish prints to make a really fishy quilt.

Fish Blocks

Note: Divide scraps into nine sets of two fabrics each. Designate one color of each set Color 1 and the remaining one Color 2.

Step 1. Cut fabric as follows for each fish: Color 1—five 2" x 2" squares; Color 2—four 2" x 2" squares, two 2 3/4" x 2 3/4" squares, one each pieces A and AR; dark aqua—1 each pieces A and AR; light aqua—two rectangles 2 3/4" x 7 1/4".

Figure 1
Sew Colors 1 and 2 squares together to make rows.

Step 2. Sew 2" Color 1 and Color 2 squares together to make three rows of three squares each as shown in Figure 1; press seam allowance toward darker fabric. Sew rows together to make Nine-Patch blocks as shown in Figure 2.

Figure 2
Join rows to make Nine-Patch blocks.

Step 3. Sew a Color 2 piece A to a dark aqua A; repeat with Color 2 piece AR and dark aqua AR pieces as shown in Figure 3. Press seam allowance toward darker fabric. Sew one 2 3/4" Color 2 square to dark aqua end of AR unit; press seams toward pieced unit.

Step 4. Sew the remaining pieced A unit to the pieced Nine-Patch referring to Figure 4 for color placement;

Project Specifications

Skill Level: Beginner
Project Size: 43 1/4" x 48 1/4"
Block Size: 9" x 9"
Number of Blocks: 9

Materials

- ✓ 1 1/2 yards light aqua print
- ✓ 3/4 yard dark aqua print
- ✓ Scraps in deep tropical colors: 1 light and 1 medium/dark per fish (18 total)
- ✓ Backing 48" x 52"
- ✓ Batting 48" x 52"
- ✓ All-purpose thread to match fabrics
- ✓ 9 black 5/8" buttons
- ✓ 5 1/2 yards self-made or purchased binding
- ✓ Basic sewing supplies and tools

press seams toward A unit. Sew the AR unit with square to the adjacent side of the pieced Nine-Patch referring to Figure 4; press seams toward A unit.

Figure 3
Join A and AR pieces as shown.

Figure 4
Sew units to pieced Nine-Patch.

Step 5. Sew one 2 3/4" x 7 1/4" light aqua rectangle to one side of pieced section; press seams toward strip. Sew a 2 3/4" x 2 3/4" Color 2 square to one end of a

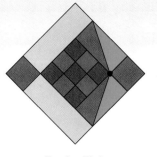

Funky Fish
9" x 9" Block

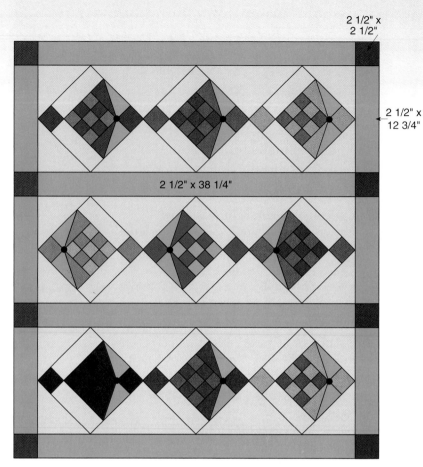

2 1/2" x
2 1/2"

2 1/2" x
12 3/4"

2 1/2" x 38 1/4"

Funky Fish Lap Quilt
Placement Diagram
43 1/4" x 48 1/4"

second light aqua rectangle and sew to pieced section as shown in Figure 5; press seams toward aqua strip. Repeat for nine blocks.

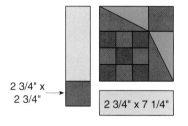

2 3/4" x
2 3/4"

2 3/4" x 7 1/4"

Figure 5
Sew pieces to pieced unit.

Top Assembly

Step 1. Cut the following: three squares light aqua 14" x 14" and six squares 7 1/4" x 7 1/4"; seven strips dark aqua 3" by fabric width; and eight 3" x 3" squares purple (or use any color from your scraps to coordinate with fish).

Step 2. Cut the 14" squares twice on the diagonal to make fill-in triangles and the 7 1/4" squares once on the

diagonal to make corner squares as shown in Figure 6. *Note: You should have 12 triangles of each size.*

14"

14"

7 1/4"

7 1/4"

Figure 6
Cut squares as shown to make triangles.

Step 3. Arrange corner and fill-in triangles with pieced squares to make a row as shown in Figure 7. Join the triangles to the squares to make a row; repeat for three

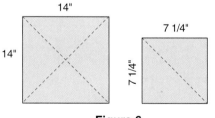

Figure 7
Arrange triangles with pieced squares to make a row.

rows. Rows should measure 13 1/4" x 38 3/4" (including seams).

Step 4. Cut four sashing strips dark aqua 3" x 38 3/4" from the cut strips; join the rows with the sashing strips beginning and ending with a strip. Press seams toward strips.

Step 5. Cut six strips dark aqua 3" x 13 1/4" from the cut strips. Sew a purple square to each end of four strips; join two of these strips with an unstitched strip to make one side border; repeat for second border. Sew to long sides of quilt center; press seams toward strips.

Step 6. Prepare top for quilting and finish referring to General Instructions. ***Note:*** *The quilt shown was machine-quilted using transparent nylon thread. The bodies of the fish were quilted as shown in Figure 8. Sashing and borders were quilted in a free-style wave pattern as shown in Figure 9. The background and remaining portions of the fish were quilted in a meandering stitch.*

Step 7. Sew one black button eye to each fish at the intersections of A and AR pieces as shown in Placement Diagram to finish.

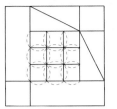

Figure 8
Quilt blocks as shown.

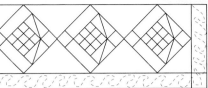

Figure 9
Quilt sashing and borders as shown.

A
Cut 2 from each Color 2 & 18 dark aqua
(reverse 1 from each Color 2 & half of dark aqua for AR)

Call of the Wild

By Connie Rand

Somewhere deep in my fabric stash lurked a large piece of wildlife print. I'm a wildlife artist myself, and I bought the print because the animal pictures were really nice. It was a long time before I actually used the fabric, since it was difficult to find a way to cut it up without losing the scenic nature of the print. Finally I found coordinating fabrics to use with it, and *Call of the Wild* was born.

Project Notes

Choose a print fabric or preprint panel that can be cut into 9 1/2" x 12 1/2" rectangles and still retain its design.

Instructions

Step 1. Cut 15 rectangles 9 1/2" x 12 1/2" from wildlife print. **Note:** *Remember that the blocks will make framed pictures, so be careful cutting the rectangles to include parts of the print that will make a good composition.*

Step 2. Cut 43 strips gold print, six strips dark blue solid and 20 strips dark green solid 1 1/2" by fabric width. Cut 15 strips gray print 3 1/2" by fabric width; subcut each gray print strip in two strips 9 1/2" and two strips 12 1/2"; repeat for 30 units of each size. Cut 60 squares 3 1/2" x 3 1/2" gold print.

Step 3. Sew a 1 1/2" gold print strip to a dark green solid strip to a gold print strip; repeat for 20 strip sets. Cut one strip set into 1 1/2" segments as shown in Figure 1. You will need 24 of these units. Cut the remaining strip sets into 9" segments as shown in Figure 2. You will need 76 of these segments.

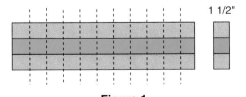

Figure 1
Cut strip set into 1 1/2" segments.

Project Specifications

Skill Level: Beginner
Quilt Size: 66" x 93"
Block Size: 15" x 18"
Number of Blocks: 15

Materials

- ✔ 2 yards wildlife print
- ✔ 3 yards gold print
- ✔ 2 yards gray print
- ✔ 1/4 yard dark blue solid
- ✔ 1 yard dark green solid
- ✔ Backing 70" x 97"
- ✔ Batting 70" x 97"
- ✔ Gray all-purpose thread
- ✔ 1 spool off-white quilting thread
- ✔ Basic sewing supplies and tools

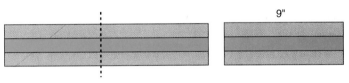

Figure 2
Cut strip set into 9" segments.

Step 4. Sew a 1 1/2" dark blue solid strip to a gold print strip to a dark blue solid strip; repeat for three strip sets. Cut strip sets into 1 1/2" segments as shown in Figure 3. You will need 86 of these segments.

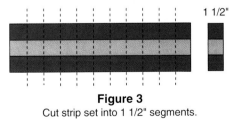

Figure 3
Cut strip set into 1 1/2" segments.

Step 5. Join two 1 1/2" blue/gold/blue segments with one 1 1/2" gold/green/gold segment to make a Nine-Patch block as shown in Figure 4; repeat for 24 blocks. Set aside remaining blue/gold/blue segments.

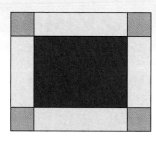

Call of the Wild
15" x 18" Block

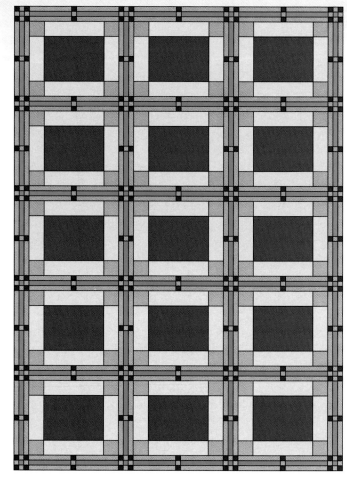

Call of the Wild
Placement Diagram
66" x 93"

Figure 4
Join 1 1/2"
segments to make a
Nine-Patch block.

Step 6. Sew a 3 1/2" gold print square to a 3 1/2" x 12 1/2" gray print strip to a gold print square. Repeat. Sew a 3 1/2" x 9 1/2" gray print strip to each side of a wildlife print rectangle. Join these units together as shown in Figure 5 to make one block; repeat for 15 blocks and press.

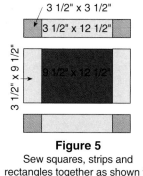

3 1/2" x 3 1/2"

3 1/2" x 12 1/2"

3 1/2" x 9 1/2"

9 1/2" x 12 1/2"

Figure 5
Sew squares, strips and
rectangles together as shown to
make 1 block.

Step 7. Sew four Nine-Patch blocks together with three 1 1/2" blue/gold/blue segments and six 9" sashing strip segments as shown in Figure 6. Repeat for six sashing rows; press.

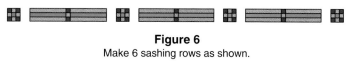

Figure 6
Make 6 sashing rows as shown.

Step 8. Sew a 1 1/2" blue/gold/blue segment between two 9" sashing strip segments as shown in Figure 7; repeat for 20 of these sashing strips.

Figure 7
Join a 1 1/2" segment with two 9"
segments to make sashing strips.

Step 9. Join four sashing strips with three wildlife blocks to make a block row as shown in Figure 8. Repeat for five rows; press.

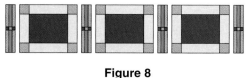

Figure 8
Make 5 block rows as shown.

Step 10. Sew sashing rows together with block rows as shown in Figure 9 to complete the top; press.

Step 11. Prepare top for quilting and finish referring to General Instructions.

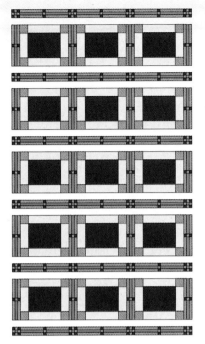

Figure 9
Arrange block rows with sashing
rows as shown; sew together to
complete quilt top.

Nouveau Nine-Patch

Continued from page 119

to make longer strips or shortened to fit the space required.

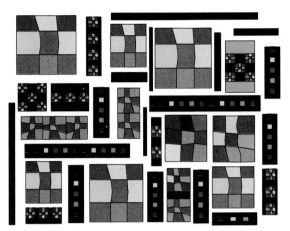

Figure 8
Arrange blocks with connector strips in a
pleasing arrangement. The drawing shows an
arrangement similar to the sample.

Assembly

Step 1. Arrange the Nine-Patch units with the connector strips in a pleasing arrangement referring to Figure 8 for suggestions. ***Note:*** *A design wall is very helpful in this instance. A makeshift design wall can be constructed from a crib-size cotton batting taped or pinned to a wall. The fabric, being cotton, adheres very nicely to cotton batting without pins and can be moved easily.*

Step 2. Beginning with the blocks of various sizes, audition spatial relationships, leaving areas free for insertion of black strips or connector strips. ***Note:*** *In this design, some of the blocks align and their seams can be matched. Others are completely askew, forming dancing Nine-Patches.*

Step 3. When a pleasing composition has been reached, begin sewing the blocks and strips together, using black strips in various widths to fill in the gaps between blocks. ***Note:*** *This quilt has a naive character that allows for uneven and non-matching size strips and blocks. A border may be added, but for a more unpredictable effect, make that border surround some blocks, leaving others free.*

Step 4. Prepare top for quilting and finish using self-made binding made from theme fabric referring to the General Instructions. ***Note:*** *The quilt shown was machine-quilted using monofilament thread. For a folk-art approach, use multicolored hand-dyed pearl cotton thread in size 8 for big-stitch hand quilting. Relax and have fun.*

Nine-Patch Cardigan Sweatshirt

By Beth Wheeler

Warm up on those cool winter days with a quilted cardigan sweatshirt. Altering a purchased pullover sweatshirt is fun and easy.

Project Notes

Choose a good quality sweatshirt of 100 percent cotton or cotton/polyester blend. Prewash and dry all fabrics; do not use fabric softener. Press to remove excess wrinkles.

Instructions

Step 1. Cut five strips blue check and four strips red check 1 1/2" by fabric width.

Step 2. Stitch strips together to make one red-blue-red and two blue-red-blue strip sets as shown in Figure 1. Cut strip sets in 1 1/2" segments.

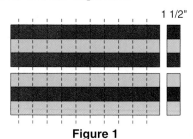

1 1/2"

Figure 1
Join strips; cut in 1 1/2" segments.

Step 3. Join segments to make 19 blocks as shown in Figure 2.

Make 19

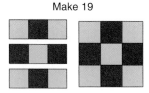

Figure 2
Join segments to make Nine-Patch blocks.

Step 4. Cut ribbing off bottom of sweatshirt. Trim with rotary cutter and ruler for a clean, even edge.

Step 5. Cut 17 squares blue stripe with red hearts 3 1/2" x 3 1/2". Join eight Nine-Patch blocks with nine

Figure 3
Join blocks and squares to make a row.

Project Specifications

Skill Level: Beginner
Sweatshirt Size: Extra-large
Block Size: 3" x 3"
Number of Blocks: 24

Materials

✔ 3/4 yard blue check
✔ 1/3 yard blue stripe with red hearts
✔ 3/4 yard red check
✔ 1 extra-large sweatshirt
✔ Coordinating all-purpose thread
✔ 1 spool clear nylon monofilament
✔ Basic sewing supplies and tools

Nine-Patch Cardigan
Placement Diagram
Extra-Large

squares to make a row referring to Figure 3; repeat for second row, alternating beginning blocks.

Step 6. Join the two rows as shown in Figure 4 to make bottom band. ***Note:*** *The number of blocks needed may vary according to the distance around the bottom edge of the chosen sweatshirt.*

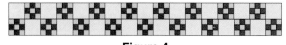

Figure 4
Join the rows to make bottom strip.

Step 7. Mark the center front of the sweatshirt; cut from bottom to top on marked line. Pin pieced panel in place along bottom cut edge of sweatshirt, beginning and ending at center front.

Step 8. Stitch along raw edges of pieced panel with a narrow zigzag stitch using monofilament thread in the top of the machine and all-purpose thread in the bobbin.

Step 9. Prepare 6 yards self-made bias binding from red check referring to General Instructions, cutting fabric 1 1/4" wide instead of 2" wide.

Step 10. Cut a length of binding long enough to fit around top edge of pieced panel. Fold under one raw edge 1/2"; press. Position other long edge of binding along raw edge of top panel edge, right sides together.

Step 11. Stitch; press up. Stitch along fold with a straight stitch using coordinating thread or a zigzag stitch using monofilament thread.

Step 12. Fold remaining binding in half along length with wrong sides together; press.

Continued on page 134

Storm at Sea

By Lucy A. Fazely

Center a lighthouse preprint panel inside the Storm at Sea design to create a pretty wall quilt for any sea-loving sailor. The design gives an illusion of movement much like the waves of the ocean.

Center Squares

Step 1. Cut the following strips across the width of the fabric: two strips light blue 2 1/2" wide; two strips dark blue 2 3/4" wide; and three strips dark blue 3 1/8" wide.

Step 2. Cut the following squares from the strips: 32 squares light blue 2 1/2" x 2 1/2"; 16 squares dark blue 2 3/4" x 2 3/4"; and 32 squares dark blue 3 1/8" x 3 1/8".

Step 3. Cut the 32 light blue 2 1/2" squares and the 32 dark blue 3 1/8" squares in half on one diagonal as shown in Figure 1.

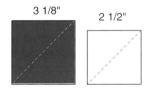

3 1/8"   2 1/2"

Figure 1
Cut squares in half on the diagonal.

Step 4. Sew a light blue triangle to each side of the 2 3/4" dark blue squares as shown in Figure 2. Sew a dark blue triangle to each side of this unit as shown in Figure 3 to complete center units.

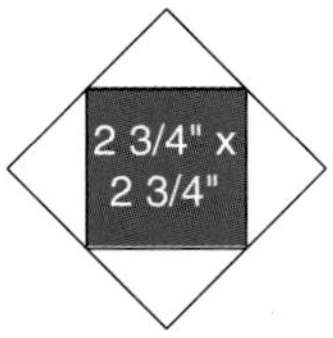

2 3/4" x 2 3/4"

Figure 2
Sew a light blue triangle to each side of the 2 3/4" dark blue squares.

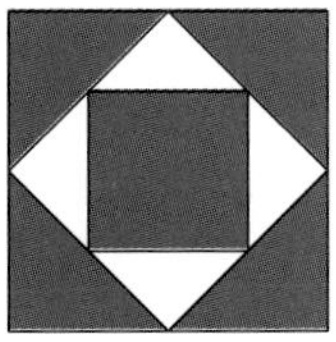

Figure 3
Sew a dark blue triangle to each side of the pieced unit.

Corner Squares

Step 1. Cut two strips light blue 2 1/8" by fabric width. Cut three strips dark blue 2" by fabric width.

Project Specifications

Skill Level: Intermediate
Quilt Size: 38" x 38"
Block Size: 9" x 9"
Number of Blocks: 8 whole blocks and 8 partial blocks

Materials

- ✔ 1 lighthouse pillow panel at least 17 1/2" x 17 1/2"
- ✔ 1 yard light blue print
- ✔ 1 1/2 yards dark blue print
- ✔ 1 1/2 yards fabric for backing and hanging sleeve
- ✔ Batting 42" x 42"
- ✔ All-purpose thread to match fabric
- ✔ Basic sewing supplies and tools

Step 2. From these strips cut the following: 32 squares light blue 2 1/8" x 2 1/8"; and 64 squares dark blue 2" x 2".

Step 3. Cut each of the 2" dark blue squares in half on the diagonal.

Step 4. Sew a dark blue triangle to each side of the light blue squares as shown in Figure 4.

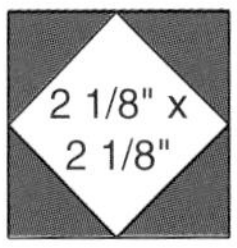

2 1/8" x 2 1/8"

Figure 4
Sew a dark blue triangle to each side of the light blue squares.

Crossbar Rectangles

Step 1. Cut the following strips across the width of the fabric: nine strips light blue 1 7/8"; and four strips dark blue 2 1/2".

Step 2. From the 1 7/8"-wide light blue strips, cut 96 rectangles light blue 1 7/8" x 3 5/8" (or use templates 1

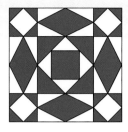

Storm at Sea
9" x 9" Block

Storm at Sea
Placement Diagram
38" x 38"

and 2 on strips). With half of the rectangles right side up and half right side down, cut the rectangles in half on the diagonal. ***Note:*** *If you rotary-cut your fabric when it was folded in half, the strips are already stacked half up and half down.*

Step 3. Using the templates given, trim the points from half of the triangles with template 1 and half with template 2. ***Note:*** *This step helps in matching pieces when stitching angled points.*

Step 4. Lay out each of the 2 1/2" dark blue strips on a flat surface. Using the diamond template given, cut the end off each strip as shown in Figure 5. Measuring from the cut angle, cut 48 diamonds each 2 1/2" wide, or use the template given to cut using traditional methods.

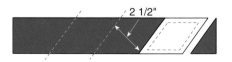

Figure 5
Cut the end off strip using diamond
template to make proper angle.

Step 5. Sew template 1 pieces to two opposite sides of each diamond as shown in Figure 6. Use the ends where you cut the points from and line the fabric up with the wide points of the diamonds; stitch. Press seams and trim excess seam allowance from points. ***Note:*** *At this point, half of the pieces will have the light blue triangles on the opposite side of the diamonds.*

Figure 6
Sew template 1 pieces to 2
opposite sides of a
diamond piece.

Figure 7
Sew template 2
pieces to diamond to
complete a 2 3/4" x
5" rectangle unit.

Step 6. Sew template 2 pieces to the remaining edges of the diamond to complete the rectangle units as shown in Figure 7. If necessary, trim rectangles to 2 3/4" x 5".

Assembly

Step 1. Using previously stitched units, piece 16 Unit 1 sections as shown in Figure 8.

Step 2. Piece 16 Unit 2 sections as shown in Figure 9.

Unit 1

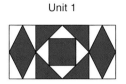

Unit 2

Figure 8
Piece 16 Unit 1 sections.

Figure 9
Piece 16 Unit 2 sections.

Step 3. Sew two Unit 2 sections to one Unit 1 as shown in Figure 10 to complete one block; repeat for eight blocks.

Figure 10
Join 1 Unit 1 and 2 Unit 2 sections to complete 1 block.

Step 4. Join three blocks and two Unit 1 sections to make the top row as shown in Figure 11; repeat for bottom row.

Figure 11
Join 3 blocks with 2 Unit 1 sections to make the top row.

Figure 12
Sew a Unit 1 section to 2 opposite sides of 1 block.

Step 5. Sew two Unit 1 sections to each side of one pieced block to make a side row as shown in Figure 12; repeat.

Step 6. Trim pillow panel to 17 1/2" x 17 1/2". Cut two strips dark blue print 1" x 17 1/2". Sew a strip to opposite sides of the panel as shown in Figure 13; press. Cut two more strips dark blue print 1" x 18 1/2"; sew to top and bottom and press.

Figure 13
Sew pieced sections and strips to center panel as shown.

Step 7. Sew the units pieced in Step 5 to the sides of the preprinted 17 1/2" x 17 1/2" panel referring to Figure 13; press seams.

Step 8. Sew the units pieced in Step 4 to the top and bottom of the pieced section referring to Figure 13; press seams.

Step 9. Cut two strips dark blue print 1 1/2" x 36 1/2". Sew a strip to opposite sides of pieced section referring to Figure 13; press. Cut two more strips 1 1/2" x 38 1/2". Sew to top and bottom of pieced section referring to Figure 13; press.

Step 10. Cut a piece of backing fabric 44" x 44".

133

Step 11. Prepare for quilting and finish edges with dark blue print referring to General Instructions for suggestions.

Step 12. Add a hanging sleeve if desired referring to page 159 for instructions.

Diamond Template
Cut 48 dark blue print

Template 2
Cut 96 light blue print

Template 1
Cut 96 light blue print

Nine-Patch Cardigan Sweatshirt
Continued from page 129

Step 13. Position raw edges of binding along right side of raw edge of sweatshirt; pin. Stitch all around, pivoting at corners to miter.

Step 14. Fold binding to inside, encasing raw edges and mitering corners. Stitch in place by hand or machine using monofilament thread.

Step 15. Cut 23 red check and 22 blue stripe squares 1 1/2" x 1 1/2". Make Nine-Patch blocks for appliqué referring to Figure 5.

Step 16. Make 1 1/3 yards bias binding, cut 1 1/4" wide, from blue check; bind edges of X blocks made in Step 15. Bind edges of O blocks made in Step 15 and the two remaining Nine-Patch blocks from Step 3 using leftover red check binding.

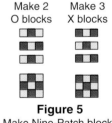

Make 2 O blocks   Make 3 X blocks

Figure 5
Make Nine-Patch blocks for appliqué as shown.

Step 17. Position one block on each elbow and remaining blocks on shirt front referring to photo and Placement Diagram for positioning suggestions. Stitch in place using a straight stitch and coordinating thread.

Step 18. Press entire cardigan for a clean, fresh look.

Quilter's Tote

By Beth Wheeler

Make a tote that will hold all of your quilting supplies for on-the-go projects or to carry materials to classes.

Project Notes

Prewash and dry all fabrics, using no fabric softener. Press to remove excess wrinkles. Stitch with a 1/4" seam allowance, unless otherwise noted.

Instructions

Step 1. Cut three strips each pink plaid and multicolored print 1 1/2" by fabric width. Join strips as shown in Figure 1; cut strip sets in 1 1/2" segments. Join segments to make Nine-Patch blocks as shown in Figure 2; repeat for nine blocks.

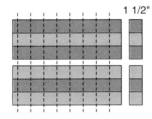

Figure 1
Join strips; cut in 1 1/2" segments.

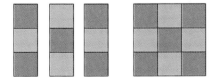

Figure 2
Join segments to make Nine-Patch
blocks.

Step 2. Cut one strip pink plaid and two strips blue check 1 1/2" by fabric width. Sew pink plaid strip between blue check strips; press seams toward blue strips. Cut strip in 3 1/2" segments as shown in Figure 3. You will need 12 segments for Rail blocks.

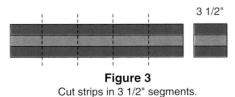

Figure 3
Cut strips in 3 1/2" segments.

Project Specifications

Skill Level: Intermediate

Tote Size: 19" x 23"

Block Size: 3" x 3"

Number of Blocks: 4 Spools, 9 Nine-Patch and 12 Rails

Materials

- 1 1/2 yards blue check
- 1/4 yard pink plaid
- 1/8 yard yellow print
- 1 yard multicolored print (includes lining)
- 1 yard fusible fleece
- Coordinating all-purpose thread
- 4 yards 1"-wide white webbing
- 2 packages large white piping
- Basic sewing supplies and tools

Step 3. Cut eight each blue check and yellow print squares 1 7/8" x 1 7/8".

Step 4. Place one blue check square on one yellow print square, right sides together. Mark a diagonal line as shown in Figure 4. Stitch 1/4" away from the line on both sides. Cut along line; press blocks open.

Figure 4
Stitch squares 1/4" away
from diagonal line.

Step 5. Cut one strip each blue check and yellow print 1 1/2" by fabric width. Cut 10 squares from each strip 1 1/2" x 1 1/2".

Step 6. Stitch squares and triangle/squares together to make two Spool A blocks and two Spool B blocks as shown in Figure 5.

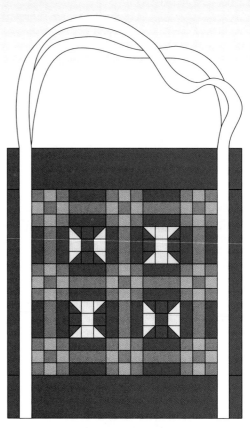

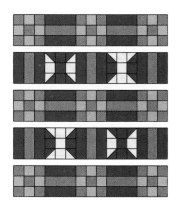

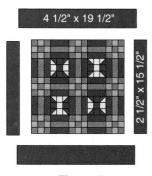

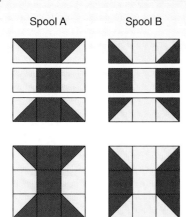

Spool A   Spool B

Figure 5
Assemble 2 spool A and 2 Spool B blocks.

Step 7. Arrange the pieced blocks in rows as shown in Figure 6. Join blocks in rows; join rows to complete pieced panel.

Figure 6
Arrange blocks in rows.

Step 8. Cut two strips blue check 2 1/2" x 15 1/2" and two strips 4 1/2" x 19 1/2".

Step 9. Sew a 2 1/2" x 15 1/2" strip to each side and a 4 1/2" x 19 1/2" strip to the top and bottom of the pieced section as shown in Figure 7.

4 1/2" x 19 1/2"

2 1/2" x 15 1/2"

Figure 7
Sew strips to pieced section as shown.

Quilter's Tote
Placement Diagram
19" x 23"

Spool A
3" x 3" Block

Spool B
3" x 3" Block

Nine-Patch
3" x 3" Block

Assembly

Step 1. Cut two 2 1/2" by fabric width strips blue check. Join strips on short ends to make a long strip for side piece. Press seam allowance open. Mark center of strip with a pin. Cut one piece of fleece the same length.

Step 2. Using pieced section as a pattern, cut one piece blue check for back, two pieces fusible fleece and two pieces multicolored print for lining. Cut two squares blue check and one square fusible fleece 11" x 11" for pocket.

Step 3. Fuse fleece to the wrong side of one pocket piece. Place pocket pieces together, right sides facing. Stitch around all outside edges, leaving a 3" opening for turning. Clip corners; turn right side out. Hand-stitch opening closed; press.

Step 4. Position pocket on tote back in position you like; stitch in place, leaving top open.

Step 5. Bond fleece pieces to corresponding front, back and side-strip pieces, trimming fleece short of seam allowances.

Step 6. Stitch side strip between front and back, centering strip on both pieces at bottom and inserting piping in both side seams and bottom seam of front only; press. Stitch piping around top edge of front.

Step 7. Cut two strips 2 1/2" by fabric width multicolored print. Join on short ends to make a long strip. Center strip between lining front and lining back, right sides together, as for tote outside. Stitch strip to front and then back to join pieces.

Finishing

Step 1. Pin webbing in place on outside of bag, positioning to cover front seam and beginning at bottom of inserted side piece. Pin up one side of the front, leaving 23" for one handle. Pin down the other side of the front; repeat for back. Turn raw end under slightly to overlap at beginning and end. Trim excess, if necessary.

Step 2. Stitch webbing in place close to both edges on webbing using coordinating thread.

Step 3. Placed pieced bag inside lining (lining is still wrong side out). *Note: Pin webbing handles down; do not include in stitching around top edge.* Stitch around top edge, leaving an opening for turning. Turn right side out; hand-stitch opening closed to finish.

Nine-Patch Purse

By Beth Wheeler

A quilter's wardrobe isn't complete without some quilted accessories. Make this easy-to-stitch purse to coordinate with quilted wearables and be the envy of your most stylish friends.

Project Notes

Prewash and dry all fabrics, using no fabric softener. Press to remove excess wrinkles. Stitch with a 1/4" seam allowance, unless otherwise noted.

If you have a problem maneuvering the purse under the sewing machine while stitching handles in place, turn entire purse inside out.

Instructions

Step 1. Cut three strips each 1 1/2" by fabric width red heart print, red plaid, red-and-blue print and red-and-blue plaid.

Step 2. Stitch a red-and-blue plaid strip to a red heart print strip to a red-and-blue plaid strip. Stitch a red heart print strip to a red-and-blue plaid strip to a red heart print strip. Stitch a red-and-blue print strip to a red plaid strip to a red-and-blue print strip. Stitch a red plaid strip to a red-and-blue print strip to a red plaid strip. Press seams in one direction on each strip set.

Step 3. Cut each strip set into 1 1/2" segments. Stitch segments together as shown in Figure 1 to make a Nine-Patch block; press. Repeat for six blocks in each color configuration.

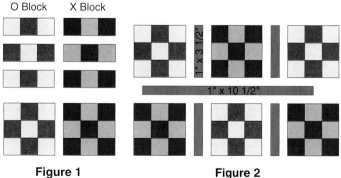

Figure 1
Join segments to make a
Nine-Patch block.

Figure 2
Stitch blocks together with
sashing strips as shown.

Project Specifications

Skill Level: Intermediate
Purse Size: Approximately 10 1/2" high, 14" wide and 6" deep
Block Size: 3" x 3"
Number of Blocks: 12

Materials

- ✔ 1/2 yard red heart print
- ✔ 1/8 yard each red plaid and red-and-blue plaid
- ✔ 1/4 yard blue stripe
- ✔ 1 yard red-and-blue print (includes lining)
- ✔ 1 yard fusible fleece
- ✔ Coordinating all-purpose thread
- ✔ 1 red 14" jacket zipper with large teeth
- ✔ Small red tassel
- ✔ Basic sewing supplies and tools

Step 4. Cut two 1" by fabric width strips blue stripe for sashing. Cut strips in eight 3 1/2" segments and two 10 1/2" segments for sashing.

Step 5. Join three blocks with 1" x 3 1/2" sashing strips to make a row as shown in Figure 2; repeat for two rows, again referring to Figure 2. Join the rows with the 1" x 10 1/2" strip to make a panel; press. Repeat for second panel.

Step 6. Cut two strips 2 1/2" by fabric width from red heart print for borders. Cut strips in four 7" segments and four 14 1/2" segments. Sew a 7" piece along short ends of one pieced panel; press seams toward strips. Sew 14 1/2" pieces to top and bottom; press seams toward strips. Repeat for second panel.

Step 7. Cut two 3 1/2" x 14 1/2" strips from red heart print for bag

Figure 3
Join pieces as shown.

top. Fold under 1" along one long edge of each piece. Insert zipper between folded edges, cutting off any excess, according to manufacturer's instructions. Stitch along both edges to hold zipper in place.

Step 8. Cut one 6" x 14 1/2" piece from red-and-blue print for bottom. Cut four end pieces from red-and-blue print, using pattern given (two will be used for lining).

Step 9. Cut two end pieces from fleece using pattern given.

Step 10. Place fleece on wrong side of corresponding fabric pieces. Trim edges away from seam allowances; fuse in place following manufacturer's directions.

Step 11. Referring to Figure 3, stitch top piece (with zipper) to the front pieced panel; add bottom and second panel. Press seam allowances in one direction.

Step 12. Cut three strips 2" by fabric width blue stripe

for handles. Stitch strips together along short ends to create one long strip; trim to approximately 112" long.

Step 13. Fold in half lengthwise right sides together; stitch along long edge. Turn right side out; press flat with seam along center back.

Step 14. From stitched strip, cut two 4" pieces of blue stripe for tabs. Fold each tab in half. Pin raw edges of each tab even with raw edges at each end of zipper; baste.

Step 15. Measure pieced section. Using this measurement, cut a piece of fleece and lining, adding an extra 1/2" to each short end of lining to turn under along zipper edge. Trim batting piece to fit up to edge of zipper Fuse in place on wrong side of pieced section.

Step 16. Fold 1" under along one short end of lining fabric; stitch to edge of zipper tape for lining. Smooth

Nine-Patch Purse
Placement Diagram
Approximately 10 1/2" high, 14" wide and 6" deep

lining flat against fleece with outside edges even; pin or baste to hold. Fold under remaining 1" on other short end; stitch to other zipper tape.

Step 17. Pin handles on the right side of the pieced panel, beginning at center bottom and covering sashing strips between Nine-Patch blocks as shown in Figure 4. Position handles across bottom, up the front along one sashing strip to the purse top, leaving 30" free for handle. Repeat around the back, leaving 30" for second handle and returning to the beginning point. Turn raw end under.

Step 18. Stitch handle strips to purse through all layers.

Step 19. Layer side pieces with batting piece between. Pin to shell, right sides facing, easing bag sides and bottom along edges of side piece. Stitch; bind inside raw edges with strips of bias cut from lining fabric to provide a clean finish for inside of bag.

Step 20. Tie a knot in the handles for strength and to control handle length. Insert a small tassel through the hole in zipper pull tab to finish.

Figure 4
Pin handles to pieced panel as shown.

Place line on fold

Side Pattern
Cut 4 red-and-blue print & 2 fleece

140

Contemporary Nine-Patch

By Janice McKee

Nine blocks make up this whole quilt. Each block is created with batik covered with meandering bias strips. Try something different to create a whole new look for the Nine-Patch tradition.

Making Narrow Bias Strips

Step 1. Fold 6" square fabric scrap on the true bias and press.

Step 2. Cut along the pressed line as shown in Figure 1. Fold again 1/4" or more along the cut edge to the wrong side of the fabric. Press and fold again the same width; press again as shown in Figure 2.

Figure 1
Fold square; cut along bias diagonal.

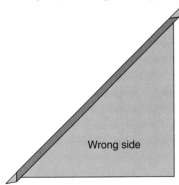
Wrong side

Figure 2
Fold cut edge 1/4" to wrong side; fold 1/4" again.

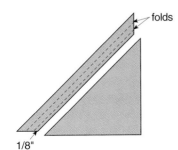
folds

1/8"

Figure 3
Cut 1/8" from second folded edge.

Project Specifications

Skill Level: Intermediate
Quilt Size: 23 1/2" x 23 1/2"
Block Size: 4 1/2" x 4 1/2"
Number of Blocks: 9

Materials

- ✔ 9 squares batik 5" x 5"
- ✔ 3/4 yard gray/black print
- ✔ 1/4 yard black solid
- ✔ 6" x 6" square (or larger) scraps assorted metallic, multicolored or strong geometric prints
- ✔ Narrow bias strips from assorted prints
- ✔ 1 spool each black and gray all-purpose thread
- ✔ 1 spool transparent nylon monofilament
- ✔ Basic sewing supplies and tools

Step 3. Cut 1/8" away from the folded edge as shown in Figure 3; press again. This creates a very narrow bias strip.

Step 4. Create as many strips as desired in various lengths. ***Note:*** *Each block of the sample quilt has at least six different bias strips.*

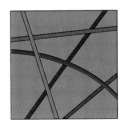

Figure 4
Lay bias strips on a square
in a pleasing arrangement.

Completing Quilt

Step 1. Cut a 26" x 26" square gray print for backing. From the remaining gray print, cut 12 strips 1 1/2" x 5" and four strips 1 1/2" x 18" for sashing.

Step 2. Lay bias strips on one 5" x 5" square in a

141

pleasing arrangement (curves, angles, straight lines) as shown in Figure 4.

Step 3. Using monofilament thread in the top of the sewing machine and gray thread in the bobbin and a zigzag stitch, stitch through the center of each bias strip to hold in place. Repeat for all 5" squares.

Step 4. Arrange three blocks with four 1 1/2" x 5" strips to make a row as shown in Figure 5; join to make a row. Press; repeat for three rows.

Step 5. Join the rows with the 1 1/2" x 18" sashing strips, beginning and ending with a strip, to complete quilt center; press.

Step 6. Cut two strips black 3 1/2" x 18"; sew to opposite sides of quilt center. Press seams toward strips. Cut two strips black 3 1/2" x 24"; sew to top and bottom. Press seams toward strips.

Step 7. Finish as directed in General Instructions, using backing folded to the front as the edge finish. ***Note:*** *The sample was machine-quilted in the ditch of blocks and sashing. Sashing strip lines were continued to quilt edges with quilting lines as shown on the Placement Diagram.*

3" x 23 1/2"

1" x 17 1/2"

1" x 4 1/2"

3" x 17 1/2"

Contemporary Nine-Patch
Placement Diagram
23 1/2" x 23 1/2"

Chambray Skirt & Vest

By Ann Boyce

The casual look is in, and what better fabric than chambray to use in clothing? Combine a variety of plaids and stripes in the blue color family to make this comfortable and stylish outfit, which would fit in almost anywhere.

Instructions

Note: One hundred percent cotton chambray was used in the sample projects. Because chambray frays when washed, zigzagging or serging seams is recommended to prevent raveling.

Skirt

Step 1. Cut one strip plaid A 14" x 60"; cut two strips plaid B 6 1/2" x 60". Cut three strips stripe A 6 1/2" x 60". Cut one 3 1/2" x 60" strip of each of the nine 1/8-yard remaining stripes and plaids. Cut each strip into 3 1/2" segments.

Step 2. Cut three strips each plaids A and B 7 1/8" by fabric width. Cut 14 triangles 10" on each square side from each fabric as shown in Figure 1.

Figure 1
Cut 10" triangles from strips.

Figure 2
Arrange stripe and plaid
squares to make a
Nine-Patch block as shown.

Project Specifications

Skill Level: Intermediate
Skirt Size: Size varies
Vest Size: Size varies
Block Size: 9" x 9"
Number of Blocks: 14 for skirt; 2 for vest

Materials

Note: Yardage given requires 60"-wide fabric.
- 1/2 yard each plaid A, plaid B and plaid C
- 1/8 yard each 4 different plaids
- 1/8 yard each 5 different stripes
- 2/3 yard stripe A
- 1 yard 1"-wide elastic
- Spray starch
- Light blue all-purpose thread
- Commercial vest pattern with no darts
- Basic sewing supplies and tools, rotary cutter, ruler and cutting mat

Step 3. Make 14 Nine-Patch blocks from the 3 1/2" cut squares, arranging plaids and stripes as shown in Figure 2; press. Set remaining squares aside for vest.

Step 4. Turn a Nine-Patch block on point; sew a plaid A triangle to one side and a plaid B triangle to the opposite side as shown in Figure 3; repeat for all Nine-Patch blocks.

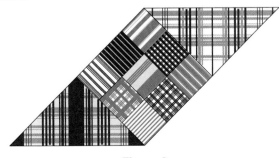

Figure 3
Sew a triangle to opposite sides of a Nine-Patch block.

Step 5. Join the stitched units together to form a tube as shown in Figure 4.

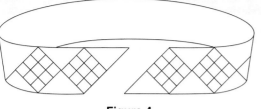

Figure 4
Join stitched units together to form a tube.

Step 6. Stitch the 14" x 60" plaid A strip edges together along the 14" side to make a tube. Turn under one 60" edge 1/2"; press. Turn under again 1 1/2"; press. Sew along turned edge to make casing for elastic, leaving 2" unstitched.

Step 7. Cut a piece of elastic your waist measurement. Put a safety pin through one end. Slide into casing through opening and pull through, holding unpinned end. When elastic emerges on the other end, remove safety pin and pin the elastic right sides together; stitch and stitch again to secure. Stitch opening on casing closed.

Step 8. Sew the 6 1/2" x 60" plaid B strip edges together along short ends to make a tube. Gather and sew one edge to the unstitched edge of the 14" piece with elastic; press.

Step 9. Join the three strips stripe A on short ends to make a tube. Sew to one edge of pieced Nine-Patch tube section, adjusting to fit, if necessary.

Step 10. Run two lines of gathering stitches along the top edge of the stitched Nine-Patch tube. Pull threads to gather to fit the unstitched edge of the plaid B top piece. Sew with right sides together, adjusting gathers to fit.

Step 11. Turn up bottom edge of stripe edge 1/4"; press. Turn up 3/4"; press. Stitch all around to form skirt hem.

Wrinkling Skirt

Step 1. Wash skirt in the quick cycle in your washer.

Step 2. Spray skirt with starch.

Step 3. Twist entire skirt in one direction until it turns into a twisted ball. Let set on the washer for one or two days.

Step 4. Carefully open skirt; spray-starch again and scrunch it together. Hang on a skirt hanger another day to dry. Do not pull the skirt outward or sideways while drying.

Chambray Vest
Placement Diagram
Size Varies

Vest

Note: Purchase an extra 1/2 yard of stripe and plaid for the top and bottom pieces on Nine-Patch blocks and yardage called for on pattern for vest lining and back.

Step 1. Make two Nine-Patch blocks as in Step 3 for skirt.

Step 2. Cut two triangles each from plaid A and plaid C as in Step 2 for skirt. Cut each triangle in half from the diagonal edge to the corner to make smaller triangles as shown in Figure 5.

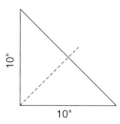

Figure 5
Cut triangles from diagonal edge to corner.

Figure 6
Sew smaller triangles to Nine-Patch block.

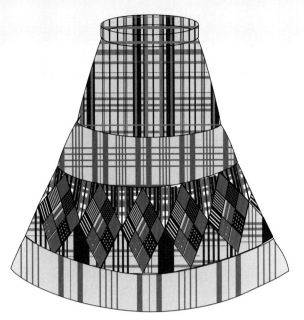

Chambray Skirt
Placement Diagram
Size Varies

Step 3. Sew a plaid A triangle to adjacent sides of a Nine-Patch block as shown in Figure 6; repeat with plaid C triangles on remaining sides. Repeat for second block.

Step 4. Lay Nine-Patch section on a flat surface. Place commercial vest front pattern on top. Cut pieces of stripe A to extend the Nine-Patch section to fit vest pattern as shown in Figure 7. Sew stripe pieces to Nine-Patch sections.

Step 5. Cut vest fronts from the pieced sections. ***Note:*** *The vest shown does not have symmetrical fronts. If you prefer the matched look, be careful to place the pattern in the same place on each stitched section so right and left sides will be the same.*

Step 6. Complete vest following instructions given with pattern to finish.

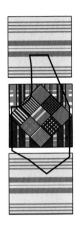

Figure 7
Sew pieces to top
and bottom of
Nine-Patch blocks
to fit vest shape.

General Instructions

Quiltmaking Basics
Materials & Supplies

Fabrics

Fabric Choices. Nine-Patch quilts combine fabrics of many types, depending on the quilt. It is best to combine same-fiber-content fabrics when making Nine-Patch quilts.

Buying Fabrics. One hundred percent cotton fabrics are recommended for making quilts. Choose colors similar to those used in the quilts shown or colors of your own preference. Most Nine-Patch quilt designs depend more on contrast of values than on the colors used to create the design.

Preparing the Fabric for Use. Fabrics may be prewashed or not depending on your preference. Whether you do or don't, be sure your fabrics are colorfast and won't run onto each other when washed after use.

Fabric Grain. Fabrics are woven with threads going in a crosswise and lengthwise direction. The threads cross at right angles—the more threads per inch, the stronger the fabric.

The crosswise threads will stretch a little. The lengthwise threads will not stretch at all. Cutting the fabric at a 45-degree angle to the crosswise and lengthwise threads produces a bias edge which stretches a great deal when pulled (Figure 1).

If templates are given with patterns in this book, pay careful attention to the grain lines marked with arrows. These arrows indicate that the piece should be placed on the lengthwise grain with the arrow running on one thread. Although it is not necessary to examine the fabric and find a thread to match to, it is important to try to place the arrow with the lengthwise grain of the fabric (Figure 2).

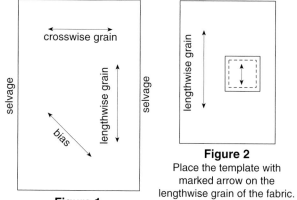

Figure 1
Drawing shows lengthwise, crosswise and bias threads.

Figure 2
Place the template with marked arrow on the lengthwise grain of the fabric.

Thread

For most piecing, good-quality cotton or cotton-covered polyester is the thread of choice. Inexpensive polyester threads are not recommended because they can cut the fibers of cotton fabrics.

Choose a color thread that will match or blend with the fabrics in your quilt. For quilts pieced with dark and light color fabrics choose a neutral thread color, such as a medium gray, as a compromise between colors. Test by pulling a sample seam.

Batting

Batting is the material used to give a quilt loft or thickness. It also adds warmth.

Batting size is listed in inches for each pattern to reflect the size needed to complete the quilt according to the instructions. Purchase the size large enough to cut the size you need for the quilt of your choice.

Some qualities to look for in batting are drapeability, resistance to fiber migration, loft and softness.

If you are unsure which kind of batting to use, purchase the smallest size batting available in the type you'd like to try. Test each sample on a small project. Choose the batting that you like working with most and that will result in the type of quilt you need.

Tools & Equipment

There are few truly essential tools and little equipment required for quiltmaking. The basics include needles (hand-sewing and quilting betweens), pins (long, thin sharp pins are best), sharp scissors or shears, a thimble, template materials (plastic or cardboard), marking tools (chalk marker, water-erasable pen and a No. 2 pencil are a few) and a quilting frame or hoop. For piecing and/or quilting by machine, add a sewing machine to the list.

Other sewing basics such as a seam ripper, pincushion, measuring tape and an iron are also necessary. For choosing colors or quilting designs for your quilt, or for designing your own quilt, it is helpful to have on hand graph paper, tracing paper, colored pencils or markers and a ruler.

For making Nine-Patch quilts, a rotary cutter, mat and specialty rulers are often used. We recommend an ergonomic rotary cutter, a large self-healing mat and several rulers. If you can choose only one size, a 6" x 24" marked in 1/8" or 1/4" increments is recommended.

Construction Methods
Templates

Traditional Templates. While most quilt instructions in this book use rotary-cut strips and quick sewing methods, a few patterns require templates. Templates are like the pattern pieces used to sew a garment. They are used to cut the fabric pieces which make up the quilt top. There are two types—templates that include a 1/4" seam allowance and those that don't.

Choose the template material and the pattern. Transfer the pattern shapes to the template material with a sharp No. 2 lead pencil. Write the pattern name, piece letter or number, grain line and number to cut for one block or whole quilt on each piece as shown in Figure 3.

Figure 3
Mark each template with the pattern name and piece identification.

Some patterns require a reversed piece (Figure 4). These patterns are labeled with an R after the piece letter; for example, F and FR. To reverse a template, first cut it with the labeled side up and then with the labeled side down. Compare these to the right and left fronts of a blouse. When making a garment, you accomplish reversed pieces when cutting the pattern on two layers of fabric placed with right sides together. This can be done when cutting templates as well.

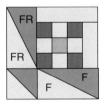

Figure 4
This pattern uses reversed pieces.

If cutting one layer of fabric at a time, first trace template onto the backside of the fabric with the marked side down; turn the template over with the marked side up to make reverse pieces.

Appliqué patterns given in this book do not include a seam allowance. Most designs are given in one drawing rather than individual pieces. This saves space while giving you the complete design to trace on the background block to help with placement of the pieces later. Make templates for each shape using the drawing for exact size. Remember to label each piece as for piecing templates.

For hand appliqué, add a seam allowance when cutting pieces from fabric. You may trace the template with label side up on the right side of the fabric if you are careful to mark lightly. The traced line is then the guide for turning the edges under when stitching.

If you prefer to mark on the wrong side of the fabric, turn the

template over if you want the pattern to face the same way it does on the page.

For machine appliqué, a seam allowance is not necessary. Trace template onto the right side of the fabric with label facing up. Cut around shape on the traced line.

Piecing

Hand-Piecing Basics. When hand-piecing it is easier to begin with templates which do not include the 1/4" seam allowance. Place the template on the wrong side of the fabric, lining up the marked grain line with lengthwise or crosswise fabric grain. If the piece does not have to be reversed, place with labeled side up. Trace around shape; move, leaving 1/2" between the shapes, and mark again.

When you have marked the appropriate number of pieces, cut out pieces, leaving 1/4" beyond marked line around each piece.

To piece, refer to assembly drawings to piece units and blocks, if provided. To join two units, place the patches with right sides together. Stick a pin in at the beginning of the seam through both fabric patches, matching the beginning points (Figure 5); for hand-piecing, the seam begins on the traced line, not at the edge of the fabric (see Figure 6).

Figure 5
Stick a pin through fabrics to match the beginning of the seam.

Figure 6
Begin hand-piecing at seam, not at the edge of the fabric. Continue stitching along seam line.

Thread a sharp needle; knot one strand of the thread at the end. Remove the pin and insert the needle in the hole; make a short stitch and then a backstitch right over the first stitch. Continue making short stitches with several stitches on the needle at one time. As you stitch, check the back piece often to assure accurate

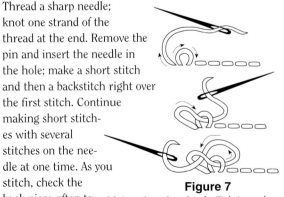

Figure 7
Make a loop in a backstitch to make a knot.

stitching on the seam line. Take a stitch at the end of the seam; backstitch and knot at the same time as shown in Figure 7.

Seams on hand-pieced fabric patches may be finger-pressed toward the darker fabric.

To sew units together, pin fabric patches together, matching seams. Sew as above except where seams meet; at these inter-sections, backstitch, go through seam to next piece and back-stitch again to secure seam joint.

Not all pieced blocks can be stitched with straight seams or in rows. Some patterns require set-in pieces. To begin a set-in seam as on a star pattern, pin one side of the square to the proper side of the star point with right sides together, matching corners. Start stitching at the seam line on the outside point; stitch on the marked seam line to the end of the seam line at the center referring to Figure 8.

Bring around the adjacent side and pin to the next star point, matching seams. Continue the stitching line from the adjacent seam through corners and to the outside edge of the square as shown in Figure 9.

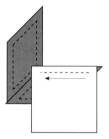 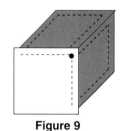

Figure 8
To set a square into a diamond point, match seams and stitch from outside edge to center.

Figure 9
Continue stitching the adjacent side of the square to the next diamond shape in 1 seam from center to outside as shown.

Machine-Piecing. If making templates, include the 1/4" seam allowance on the template for machine-piecing. Place template on the wrong side of the fabric as for hand-piecing except butt pieces against one another when tracing.

Set machine on 2.5 or 12–15 stitches per inch. Join pieces as for hand-piecing for set-in seams; but for other straight seams, begin and end sewing at the end of the fabric patch sewn as shown in Figure 10. No backstitching is necessary when machine-stitching.

Figure 10
Begin machine-piecing at the end of the piece, not at the end of the seam.

Join units as for hand-piecing referring to the piecing diagrams where needed. Chain piecing (Figure 11—sewing several like units before sewing other units) saves time by eliminating beginning and ending stitches.

When joining machine-pieced units, match seams against each other with seam allowances pressed in opposite directions to

reduce bulk and make perfect matching of seams possible (Figure 12).

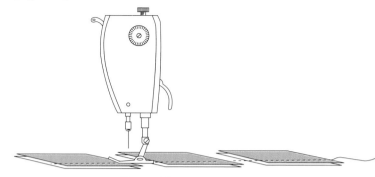

Figure 11
Units may be chain-pieced to save time.

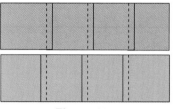

Figure 12
Sew machine-pieced units with seams pressed in opposite directions.

Cutting

Quick-Cutting. Quick-cutting and piecing strips is recom-mended for making many of the Nine-Patch quilts in this book. Templates are completely eliminated; instead, a rotary cutter, plastic ruler and mat are used to cut fabric pieces.

When rotary-cutting strips, straighten raw edges of fabric by folding fabric in fourths across the width as shown in Figure 13. Press down flat; place ruler on fabric square with edge of fabric and make one cut from the folded edge to the outside edge. If strips are not straightened, a wavy strip will result as shown in Figure 14.

Tips & Techniques

Before machine-piecing fabric patches together, test your sewing machine for positioning an accurate 1/4" seam allowance. There are several tools to help guaran-tee this. Some machine needles may be moved to allow the presser-foot edge to be a 1/4" guide.

A special foot may be purchased for your machine that will guarantee an accurate 1/4" seam. A piece of masking tape can be placed on the throat plate of your sewing machine to mark the 1/4" seam. A plastic stick-on ruler may be used instead of tape with the same results.

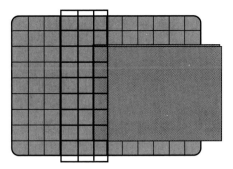

Figure 13
Fold fabric and straighten as shown.

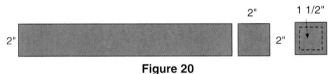

Figure 14
Wavy strips result if fabric is not straightened before cutting.

Always cut away from your body, holding the ruler firmly with the non-cutting hand. Keep fingers away from the edge of the ruler as it is easy for the rotary cutter to slip and jump over the edge of the ruler if cutting is not properly done.

For many Nine-Patch blocks three strips are stitched together—usually two from the same fabric and one from another fabric as shown in Figure 15. The strips are stitched, pressed and cut into segments. A second strip set is stitched using the same colors but reversing the order as shown in Figure 16. The sets are cut into segments as shown in Figure 17.

Figure 15
Join 3 strips as shown.

Figure 16
Sew a second strip set
with alternating colors.

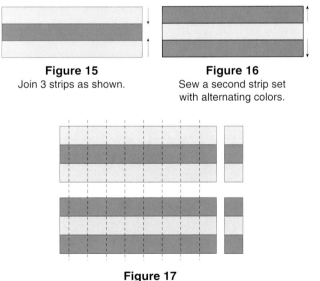

Figure 17
Cut segments from the stitched strip set.

The cut segments are arranged as shown in Figure 18 and stitched to complete one Nine-Patch block. Although the block shown is very simple, the same methods may be used for more complicated patterns.

The direction to press seams on strip sets is important for accurate piecing later. The normal rule for pressing is to press

seams toward the darker fabric to keep the colors from showing through on lighter colors later. For joining segments from strip sets, this rule doesn't always apply.

It is best if seams on adjacent rows are pressed in opposite directions. Refer to arrows on Figures 15 and 16 for suggested pressing directions. When aligning segments to stitch rows together, if pressed properly, seam joints will have a seam going in both directions as shown in Figure 19.

If a square is required for the pattern, it can be sub-cut from a strip as shown in Figure 20.

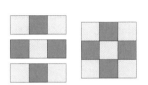

Figure 18
Arrange cut segments to
make a Nine-Patch block.

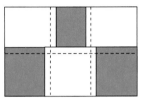

Figure 19
Seams go in both directions
at seam joints.

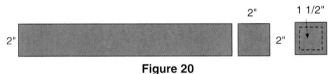

Figure 20
If cutting squares, cut proper-width strip into same-width segments. Here, a 2" strip is cut into 2" segments to create 2" squares. These squares finish at 1 1/2" when sewn.

If you need right triangles with the straight grain on the short sides, you can use the same method, but you need to figure out how wide to cut the strip. Measure the finished size of one short side of the triangle. Add 7/8" to this size for seam allowance. Cut fabric strips this width; cut the strips into the same increment to create squares. Cut the squares on the diagonal to produce triangles. For example, if you need a triangle with a 2" finished height, cut the strips 2 7/8" by the width of the fabric. Cut the strips into 2 7/8" squares. Cut each square on the diagonal to produce the correct-size triangle with the grain on the short sides (Figure 21).

Figure 21
Cut 2" (finished size) triangles from
2 7/8" squares as shown.

Triangles sewn together to make squares are called half-square triangles or triangle/squares. When joined, the triangle/square unit has the straight of grain on all outside edges of the block.

Another method of making triangle/squares is shown in Figure

22. Layer two squares with right sides together; draw a diagonal line through the center. Stitch 1/4" on both sides of the line. Cut apart on the drawn line to reveal two stitched triangle/squares.

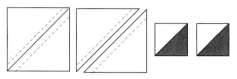

Figure 22
Mark a diagonal line on the square; stitch
1/4" on each side of the line. Cut on line
to reveal stitched triangle/squares.

If you need triangles with the straight of grain on the diagonal, such as for fill-in triangles on the outside edges of a diagonal-set quilt, the procedure is a bit different.

To make these triangles, a square is cut on both diagonals; thus, the straight of grain is on the longest or diagonal side (Figure 23). To figure out the size to cut the square, add 1 1/4" to the needed finished size of the longest side of the triangle. For example, if you need a triangle with a 12" finished diagonal, cut a 13 1/4" square.

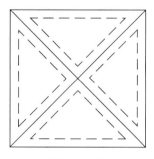

Figure 23
Add 1 1/4" to finished size of longest side of triangle needed
and cut on both diagonals to make a quarter-square triangle.

If templates are given, use their measurements to cut fabric strips to correspond with that measurement. The template may be used on the strip to cut pieces quickly. Strip cutting works best for squares, triangles, rectangles and diamonds. Odd-shaped templates are difficult to cut in multiple layers using a rotary cutter.

Foundation Piecing

Foundation Piecing. Paper or fabric foundation pieces are used to make very accurate blocks, provide stability for weak fabrics, and add body and weight to the finished quilt.

Temporary foundation materials include paper, tracing paper, freezer paper and removable interfacing. Permanent foundations include utility fabrics, non-woven interfacing, flannel, fleece and batting.

Methods of marking foundations include basting lines, pencils or pens, needlepunching, tracing wheel, hot-iron transfers, copy machine, premarked, stamps or stencils.

When foundation piecing, the pattern needs to be reversed when tracing. ***Note:*** *All patterns for which we recommend paper piecing are already reversed in full-size drawings given.*

To begin, place a scrap of fabric larger than the lined space on the unlined side of the paper in the No. 1 position. Place piece 2 right sides together with piece 1; pin on seam line, and fold back to check that the piece will cover space 2 before stitching.

Stitch along line on the lined side of the paper—fabric will not be visible. Sew several stitches beyond the beginning and ending of the line. Backstitching is not required as another fabric seam will cover this seam.

Remove pin; finger-press piece 2 flat. Continue adding all pieces in numerical order in the same manner until all pieces are stitched to paper. Trim excess to outside line (1/4" larger all around than finished size of the block).

Tracing paper can be used as a temporary foundation. It is removed when blocks are complete and stitched together. To paper-piece, copy patterns using a copy machine or trace each block individually. Measure the finished paper foundations to insure accuracy in copying.

Tips & Techniques

If you cannot see the lines on the backside of the paper when paper-piecing, draw over lines with a small felt-tip marker. The lines should now be visible on the backside to help with placement of fabric pieces.

Appliqué

Appliqué. Appliqué is the process of applying one piece of fabric on top of another for decorative or functional purposes.

Making Templates. Most appliqué designs given here are given as full-size drawings for the completed designs. The drawings show dotted lines to indicate where one piece overlaps another. Other marks indicate placement of embroidery stitches for decorative purposes such as eyes, lips, flowers, etc.

For hand appliqué, trace each template onto the right side of

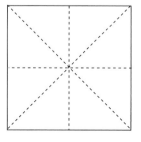

Figure 24
Fold background to mark centers as shown.

the fabric with template right side up. Cut around shape, adding a 1/8"–1/4" seam allowance.

Before the actual appliqué process begins, cut the background block and prepare it for stitching. Most appliqué designs are centered on the block. To find the center of the background square, fold it in half and in half again; crease with your fingers. Now unfold and fold diagonally and crease; repeat for other corners referring to Figure 24.

Center line creases to help position the design. If you have a full-size drawing of the design, as is given with most appliqué designs in this book, it might help you to draw on the background block to help with placement.

Transfer the design to a large piece of tracing paper. Place the paper on top of the design; use masking tape to hold in place. Trace design onto paper.

If you don't have a light box, tape the pattern on a window; center the background block on top and tape in place. Trace the design onto the background block with a water-erasable marker or chalk pencil. This drawing will mark exactly where the fabric pieces should be placed on the background block.

Hand Appliqué. Traditional hand appliqué uses a template made from the desired finished shape without seam allowance added.

After fabric is prepared, trace the desired shape onto the right side of the fabric with a water-erasable marker, light lead or chalk pencil. Leave at least 1/2" between design motifs when tracing to allow for the seam allowance when cutting out the shapes.

When the desired number of shapes needed has been drawn on the fabric pieces, cut out shapes leaving 1/8"–1/4" all around drawn line for turning under.

Turn the shape's edges over on the drawn line. When turning the edges under, make sharp corners sharp and smooth edges smooth. The fabric patch should retain the shape of the template used to cut it.

When turning in concave curves, clip to seams and baste the seam allowance over as shown in Figure 25.

During the actual appliqué process, you may be layering one shape on top of another. Where two fabrics overlap, the underneath piece does not have to be turned under or stitched down.

Figure 25
Concave curves should be clipped before turning as shown.

If possible, trim away the underneath fabric when the block is finished by carefully cutting away the background from underneath and then cutting away unnecessary layers to reduce bulk and avoid shadows from darker fabrics showing through on light fabrics.

For hand appliqué, position the fabric shapes on the background block and pin or baste them in place. Using a blind-stitch or appliqué stitch, sew pieces in place with matching thread and small stitches. Start with background pieces first and work up to foreground pieces. Appliqué the pieces in place on the background in numerical order, if given, layering as necessary.

Machine Appliqué. There are several products available to help make the machine-appliqué process easier and faster.

Fusible transfer web is a commercial product similar to iron-on interfacings except it has two sticky sides. It is used to adhere appliqué shapes to the background with heat. Paper is adhered to one side of the web.

To use, dry-iron the sticky side of the fusible product onto the wrong side of the chosen fabric. Draw desired shapes onto the paper and cut them out. Peel off the paper and dry-iron the shapes in place on the background fabric. The shape will stay in place while you stitch around it. This process adds a little bulk or stiffness to the appliquéd shape and makes quilting through the layers by hand difficult.

For successful machine appliqué a tear-off stabilizer is recommended. This product is placed under the background fabric while machine appliqué is being done. It is torn away when the work is finished. This kind of stabilizer keeps the background fabric from pulling during the machine-appliqué process.

During the actual machine-appliqué process, you will be layering one shape on top of another. Where two fabrics overlap, the underneath piece does not have to be turned under or stitched down.

Thread the top of the machine with thread to match the fabric patches or with threads that coordinate or contrast with fabrics. Rayon thread is a good choice when a sheen is desired on the finished appliqué stitches. Do not use rayon thread in the bobbin; use all-purpose thread.

Set your machine to make a zigzag stitch and practice on scraps of similar weight to check the tension. If you can see the bobbin thread on the top of the appliqué, adjust your machine to make a balanced stitch. Different-width stitches are available; choose one that will not overpower the appliqué shapes. In some cases these appliqué stitches will be used as decorative stitches as well and you may want the thread to show.

If using a stabilizer, place this under the background fabric and pin or fuse in place. Place shapes as for hand-appliqué and stitch all around shapes by machine.

When all machine work is complete, remove stabilizer from the back referring to the manufacturer's instructions.

Putting It All Together

Many steps are required to prepare a quilt top for quilting, including setting the blocks together, adding borders, choosing and marking quilting designs, layering the top, batting and backing for quilting, quilting or tying the layers and finishing the edges of the quilt.

As you begin the process of finishing your quilt top, strive for a neat, flat quilt with square sides and corners, not for perfection—that will come with time and practice.

Finishing the Top

Settings. Most quilts are made by sewing individual blocks together in rows which, when joined, create a design. There are several other methods used to join blocks. Sometimes the setting choice is determined by the block's design. For example, a house block should be placed upright on a quilt, not sideways or upside down.

Plain blocks can be alternated with pieced or appliquéd blocks in a straight set. Making a quilt using plain blocks saves time; half the number of pieced or appliquéd blocks are needed to make the same-size quilt as shown in Figure 1.

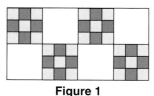

Figure 1
Alternate plain blocks with pieced blocks to save time.

Borders. Borders are an integral part of the quilt and should complement the colors and designs used in the quilt center. Borders frame a quilt just like a mat and frame do a picture.

If fabric strips are added for borders, they may be mitered or butted at the corners as shown in Figures 2 and 3. To determine the size for butted border strips, measure across the center of the completed quilt top from one side raw edge to the other side raw edge. This measurement will include a 1/4" seam allowance.

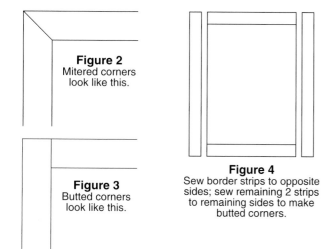

Figure 2
Mitered corners look like this.

Figure 3
Butted corners look like this.

Figure 4
Sew border strips to opposite sides; sew remaining 2 strips to remaining sides to make butted corners.

Cut two border strips that length by the chosen width of the border. Sew these strips to the top and bottom of the pieced center referring to Figure 4. Press the seam allowance toward the border strips.

Measure across the completed quilt top at the center, from top raw edge to bottom raw edge, including the two border strips already added. Cut two border strips that length by the chosen width of the border. Sew a strip to each of the two remaining sides as shown in Figure 4. Press the seams toward the border strips.

To make mitered corners, measure the quilt as before. To this add twice the width of the border and 1/2" for seam allowances to determine the length of the strips. Repeat for opposite sides. Sew on each strip, stopping stitching 1/4" from corner, leaving the remainder of the strip dangling.

Press corners at a 45-degree angle to form a crease. Stitch from the inside quilt corner to the outside on the creased line. Trim excess away after stitching and press mitered seams open (Figures 5–7).

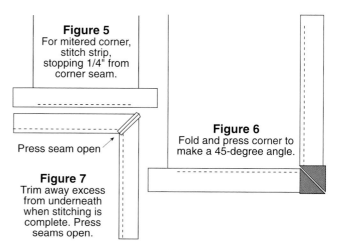

Figure 5
For mitered corner, stitch strip, stopping 1/4" from corner seam.

Press seam open

Figure 6
Fold and press corner to make a 45-degree angle.

Figure 7
Trim away excess from underneath when stitching is complete. Press seams open.

Carefully press the entire piece, including the pieced center. Avoid pulling and stretching while pressing, which would distort shapes.

Getting Ready to Quilt

Choosing a Quilting Design. If you choose to hand- or machine-quilt your finished top, you will need to choose a design for quilting.

There are several types of quilting designs, some of which may not have to be marked. The easiest of the unmarked designs is in-the-ditch quilting. Here the quilting stitches are placed in the valley created by the seams joining two pieces together or next to the edge of an appliqué design. There is no need to mark a top for in-the-ditch quilting. Machine quilters choose this option because the stitches are not as obvious on the finished quilt (Figure 8).

Outline-quilting 1/4" or more away from seams or appliqué shapes is another no-mark alternative (Figure 9) which prevents having to sew through the layers made by seams, thus making stitching easier.

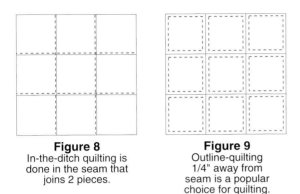

Figure 8
In-the-ditch quilting is
done in the seam that
joins 2 pieces.

Figure 9
Outline-quilting
1/4" away from
seam is a popular
choice for quilting.

If you are not comfortable eyeballing the 1/4" (or other distance), masking tape is available in different widths and is helpful to place on straight-edge designs to mark the quilting line. If using masking tape, place the tape right up against the seam and quilt close to the other edge.

Meander or free-motion quilting by machine fills in open spaces and doesn't require marking. It is fun and easy to stitch as shown in Figure 10.

Figure 10
Machine meander quilting
fills in large spaces.

Marking the Top for Quilting or Tying. If you choose a fancy or allover design for quilting, you will need to transfer the design to your quilt top before layering with the backing and batting. You may use a sharp medium-lead or silver pencil on light background fabrics. Test the pencil marks to guarantee that they will wash out of your quilt top when quilting is complete; or be sure your quilting stitches cover the pencil marks. Mechanical pencils with very fine points may be used successfully to mark quilts.

Manufactured quilt-design templates are available in many designs and sizes and are cut out of a durable plastic template material which is easy to use.

To make a permanent quilt-design template, choose a template material on which to transfer the design. See-through plastic is the best as it will let you place the design while allowing you to see where it is in relation to your quilt design without moving it. Place the design on the quilt top where you want it and trace around it with your marking tool. Pick up the quilting template and place again; repeat marking.

No matter what marking method you use, remember—the marked lines should *never show* on the finished quilt. When the top is marked, it is ready for layering.

Preparing the Quilt Backing. The quilt backing is a very important feature of your quilt. In most cases, the materials list for each quilt in this book gives the size requirements for the backing, not the yardage needed. Exceptions to this are when

the backing fabric is also used on the quilt top and yardage is given for that fabric.

A backing is generally cut at least 4" larger than the quilt top or 2" larger on all sides. For a 64" x 78" finished quilt, the backing would need to be at least 68" x 82".

To avoid having the seam across the center of the quilt backing, cut or tear one of the right-length pieces in half and sew half to each side of the second piece as shown in Figure 11.

Quilts that need a backing more than 88" wide may be pieced in horizontal pieces as shown in Figure 12.

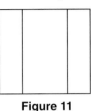

Figure 11
Center 1 backing piece with a piece on each side.

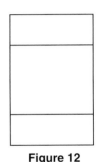

Figure 12
Horizontal seams may be used on backing pieces.

Layering the Quilt Sandwich. Layering the quilt top with the batting and backing is time-consuming. Open the batting several days before you need it and place over a bed or flat on the floor to help flatten the creases caused from its being folded up in the bag for so long.

Iron the backing piece, folding in half both vertically and horizontally and pressing to mark centers.

If you will not be quilting on a frame, place the backing right side down on a clean floor or table. Start in the center and push any wrinkles or bunches flat. Use masking tape to tape the edges to the floor or large clips to hold the backing to the edges of the table. The backing should be taut.

Place the batting on top of the backing, matching centers using fold lines as guides; flatten out any wrinkles. Trim the batting to the same size as the backing.

Fold the quilt top in half lengthwise and place on top of the batting, wrong side against the batting, matching centers. Unfold quilt and, working from the center to the outside edges, smooth out any wrinkles or lumps.

To hold the quilt layers together for quilting, baste by hand or use safety pins. If basting by hand, thread a long thin needle with a long piece of unknotted white or off-white thread. Starting in the center and leaving a long tail, make 4"–6" stitches toward the outside edge of the quilt top, smoothing as you baste. Start at the center again and work toward the outside as shown in Figure 13.

If quilting by machine, you may prefer to use safety pins for holding your fabric sandwich together. Start in the center of the quilt and pin to the outside, leaving pins open until all are placed. When you are satisfied that all layers are smooth, close the pins.

Figure 13
Baste from the center to the outside edges.

Quilting

Hand Quilting. Hand quilting is the process of placing stitches through the quilt top, batting and backing to hold them together. While it is a functional process, it also adds beauty and loft to the finished quilt.

To begin, thread a sharp between needle with an 18" piece of quilting thread. Tie a small knot in the end of the thread. Position the needle about 1/2" to 1" away from the starting point on quilt top. Sink the needle through the top into the batting layer but not through the backing. Pull the needle up at the starting point of the quilting design. Pull the needle and

Tips & Techniques

Knots should not show on the quilt top or back. Learn to sink the knot into the batting at the beginning and ending of the quilting thread for successful stitches. Making 12–18 stitches per inch is a nice goal, but a more realistic goal is seven to nine stitches per inch. If you cannot accomplish this right away, strive for even stitches—all the same size—that look as good on the back as on the front.

When you have nearly run out of thread, wind the thread around the needle several times to make a small knot and pull it close to the fabric. Insert the needle into the fabric on the quilting line and come out with the needle 1/2" to 1" away, pulling the knot into the fabric layers the same as when you started. Pull and cut thread close to fabric. The end should disappear inside after cutting. Some quilters prefer to take a backstitch with a loop through it for a knot to end.

You will perfect your quilting stitches as you gain experience, your stitches will get better with each project and your style will be uniquely your own.

thread until the knot sinks through the top into the batting (Figure 14).

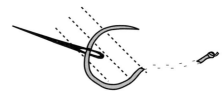

Figure 14
Start the needle through the top layer of fabric 1/2"–1" away from quilting line with knot on top of fabric.

Some stitchers like to take a backstitch here at the beginning while others prefer to begin the first stitch here. Take small, even running stitches along the marked quilting line (Figure 15). Keep one hand positioned underneath to feel the needle go all the way through to the backing.

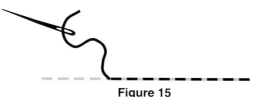

Figure 15
Make small, even running stitches on marked quilting line.

Machine Quilting. Successful machine quilting requires practice and a good relationship with your sewing machine.

Prepare the quilt for machine quilting in the same way as for hand quilting. Use safety pins to hold the layers together instead of basting with thread.

Presser-foot quilting is best used for straight-line quilting because the presser bar lever does not need to be continually lifted.

Set the machine on a longer stitch length (three or eight to 10 stitches to the inch). Too tight a stitch causes puckering and fabric tucks, either on the quilt top or backing. An even-feed or walking foot helps to eliminate the tucks and puckering by feeding the upper and lower layers through the machine evenly. Before you begin, loosen the amount of pressure on the presser foot.

Special machine-quilting needles work best to penetrate the three layers in your quilt.

Decide on a design. Quilting in the ditch is not quite as visible, but if you quilt with the feed dogs engaged, it means turning the quilt frequently. It is not easy to fit a rolled-up quilt through the small opening on the sewing machine head.

Meander quilting is the easiest way to machine-quilt—and it is fun. Meander quilting is done using an appliqué or darning foot with the feed dogs dropped. It is sort of like scribbling. Simply move the quilt top around under the foot and make stitches in a random pattern to fill the space. The same method may be used to outline a quilt design. The trick is the same as in hand-quilting; you are striving for stitches of uniform size. Your hands are in complete control of the design.

If machine-quilting is of interest to you, there are several very good books available at quilt shops that will help you become a successful machine quilter.

Tied Quilts, or Comforters. Would you rather tie your quilt layers together than quilt them? Tied quilts are often referred to as comforters. The advantage of tying is that it takes so much less time and the required skills can be learned quickly.

If a top will be tied, choose a thick, bonded batting—one that will not separate during washing. For tying, use pearl cotton, embroidery floss, or strong yarn in colors that match or coordinate with the fabrics in your quilt top.

Decide on a pattern for tying. Many quilts are tied at the corners and centers of the blocks and at sashing joints. Try to tie every 4"–6". Special designs can be used for tying, but most quilts are tied in conventional ways. Begin tying in the center and work to the outside edges.

To make the tie, thread a large needle with a long thread (yarn, floss or crochet cotton); do not knot. Push the needle through the quilt top to the back, leaving a 3"–4" length on top. Move the needle to the next position without cutting thread.
Take another stitch through the layers; repeat until thread is almost used up.

Cut thread between stitches, leaving an equal amount of thread on each stitch. Tie a knot with the two thread ends. Tie again to make a square knot referring to Figure 16. Trim thread ends to desired length.

Figure 16
Make a square knot as shown.

Tips & Techniques

Use a thimble to prevent sore fingers when hand quilting. The finger that is under the quilt to feel the needle as it passes through the backing is the one that is most apt to get sore from the pin pricks. Some quilters purchase leather thimbles for this finger while others try home remedies. One simple aid is masking tape wrapped around the finger. With the tape you will still be able to feel the needle, but it will not prick your skin. Over time calluses build up and these fingers get toughened up, but with every vacation from quilting, they will become soft and the process begins again.

When you feel your shoulder muscles tensing up, take a rest.

Finishing the Edges

After your quilt is tied or quilted, the edges need to be finished. Decide how you want the edges of your quilt finished before layering the backing and batting with the quilt top.

Without Binding—Self-Finish. There is one way to eliminate adding an edge finish. This is done before quilting. Place the

batting on a flat surface. Place the pieced top right side up on the batting. Place the backing right sides together with the pieced top. Pin and/or baste the layers together to hold flat referring to page 155.

Begin stitching in the center of one side using a 1/4" seam allowance, reversing at the beginning and end of the seam. Continue stitching all around and back to the beginning side. Leave a 12" or larger opening. Clip corners to reduce excess. Turn right side out through the opening. Slipstitch the opening closed by hand. The quilt may now be quilted by hand or machine.

The disadvantage to this method is that once the edges are sewn in, any creases or wrinkles that might form during the quilting process cannot be flattened out. Tying is the preferred method for finishing a quilt constructed using this method.

Bringing the backing fabric to the front is another way to finish the quilt's edge without binding. To accomplish this, complete the quilt as for hand or machine quilting. Trim the batting *only* even with the front. Trim the backing 1" larger than the completed top all around.

Turn the backing edge in 1/2" and then turn over to the front along edge of batting. The folded edge may be machine-stitched close to the edge through all layers, or blind-stitched in place to finish.

The front may be turned to the back. If using this method, a wider front border is needed. The backing and batting are trimmed 1" *smaller* than the top and the top edge is turned under 1/2" and then turned to the back and stitched in place.

One more method of self-finish may be used. The top and backing may be stitched together by hand at the edge. To accomplish this, all quilting must be stopped 1/2" from the quilt-top edge. The top and backing of the quilt are trimmed even and the batting is trimmed to 1/4"–1/2" smaller. The edges of the top and backing are turned in 1/4"–1/2" and blind-stitched together at the very edge.

These methods do not require the use of extra fabric and save time in preparation of binding strips; they are not as durable as an added binding.

Binding. The technique of adding extra fabric at the edges of the quilt is called binding. The binding encloses the edges and adds an extra layer of fabric for durability.

To prepare the quilt for the addition of the binding, trim the batting and backing layers flush with the top of the quilt using a rotary cutter and ruler or shears. Using a walking-foot attachment (sometimes called an even-feed foot attachment), machine-baste the three layers together all around approximately 1/8" from the cut edge.

The list of materials given with each quilt in this book often includes a number of yards of self-made or purchased binding. Bias binding may be purchased in packages and in many colors. The advantage to self-made binding is that you can use fabrics from your quilt to coordinate colors.

Double-fold, straight-grain binding and double-fold, bias-grain binding are two of the most commonly used types of binding.

Double-fold, straight-grain binding is used on smaller projects with right-angle corners. Double-fold, bias-grain binding is best suited for bed-size quilts or quilts with rounded corners.

To make double-fold, straight-grain binding, cut 2"-wide strips of fabric across the width or down the length of the fabric totaling the perimeter of the quilt plus 10". The strips are joined as shown in Figure 17 and pressed in half wrong sides together along the length using an iron on a cotton setting with *no* steam.

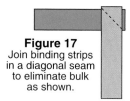

Figure 17
Join binding strips
in a diagonal seam
to eliminate bulk
as shown.

Lining up the raw edges, place the binding on the top of the quilt and begin sewing (again using the walking foot) approximately 6" from the beginning of the binding strip. Stop sewing 1/4" from the first corner, leave the needle in the quilt, turn and sew diagonally to the corner as shown in Figure 18.

Fold the binding at a 45-degree angle up and away from the quilt as shown in Figure 19 and back down flush with the raw edges. Starting at the top raw edge of the quilt, begin sewing the next side as shown in Figure 20. Repeat at the next three corners.

 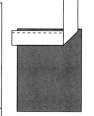

Figure 18
Sew to within 1/4" of
corner; leave needle
in quilt, turn and stitch
diagonally off the
corner of the quilt.

Figure 19
Fold binding at a
45-degree angle
up and away from
quilt as shown.

Figure 20
Fold the binding
strips back down,
flush with the raw
edge, and begin
sewing.

As you approach the beginning of the binding strip, stop stitching and overlap the binding 1/2" from the edge; trim. Join the two ends with a 1/4" seam allowance and press the seam open. Reposition the joined binding along the edge of the quilt and resume stitching to the beginning.

To finish, bring the folded edge of the binding over the raw edges and blind-stitch the binding in place over the machine-stitching line on the backside. Hand-miter the corners on the back as shown in Figure 21.

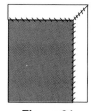

Figure 21
Miter and stitch the
corners as shown.

If you are making a quilt to be used on a bed, you will want to use double-fold, bias-grain bindings because the many threads

that cross each other along the fold at the edge of the quilt make it a more durable binding.

Cut 2"-wide bias strips from a large square of fabric. Join the strips as illustrated in Figure 17 and press the seams open. Fold the beginning end of the bias strip 1/4" from the raw edge and press. Fold the joined strips in half along the long side, wrong sides together, and press with *no* steam (Figure 22).

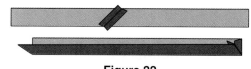

Figure 22
Fold end in and press strip in half.

Follow the same procedures as previously described for preparing the quilt top and sewing the binding to the quilt top. Treat corners just as you treated them with straight-grain binding.

Since you are using bias-grain binding, you do have the option to just eliminate the corners if this option doesn't interfere with the patchwork in the quilt. Round the corners off by placing one of your dinner plates at the corner and rotary-cutting the gentle curve (Figure 23).

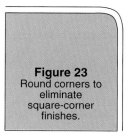

Figure 23
Round corners to
eliminate
square-corner
finishes.

As you approach the beginning of the binding strip, stop stitching and lay the end across the beginning so it will slip inside the fold. Cut the end at a 45-degree angle so the raw edges are contained inside the beginning of the strip (Figure 24). Resume stitching to the beginning. Bring the fold to the back of the quilt and hand-stitch as previously described.

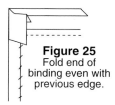

Figure 24
End the binding strips as shown.

Overlapped corners are not quite as easy as rounded ones, but a bit easier than mitering. To make overlapped corners, sew binding strips to opposite sides of the quilt top. Stitch edges down to finish. Trim ends even.

Sew a strip to each remaining side, leaving 1 1/2"–2" excess at each end. Turn quilt over and fold binding down even with previous finished edge as shown in Figure 25.

Figure 25
Fold end of
binding even with
previous edge.

Fold binding in toward quilt and stitch down as before, enclosing the previous bound edge in the seam as shown in Figure 26. It may be necessary to trim the folded-down section to reduce bulk.

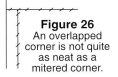

Figure 26
An overlapped corner is not quite as neat as a mitered corner.

Making Continuous Bias Binding

Instead of cutting individual bias strips and sewing them together, you may make continuous bias binding.

To make approximately 4 yards of binding, cut a square 18" x 18" from chosen binding fabric. Cut the square once on the diagonal to make two triangles as shown in Figure 27. With right sides together, sew the two triangles together with a 1/4" seam allowance as shown in Figure 28; press seam open to reduce bulk.

Mark lines every 2 1/4" on the wrong side of the fabric as shown in Figure 29. Bring the short ends together, right sides together, offsetting one line as shown in Figure 30 to make a tube. This will seam awkward.

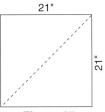

Figure 27
Cut 21" square on the diagonal.

Figure 28
Sew the triangles together.

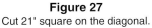

Figure 29
Mark lines every 2 1/4".

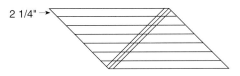

Figure 30
Sew short ends together, offsetting lines to make a tube.

Begin cutting at point A as shown in Figure 31; continue cutting along marked line to make one continuous strip. Fold strip in half along length with wrong sides together; press. Sew to quilt edges as instructed previously for bias binding.

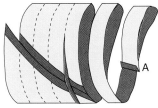

Figure 31
Cut along marked lines, starting at A.

Final Touches

If your quilt will be hung on the wall, a hanging sleeve is required. Other options include purchased plastic rings or fabric tabs. The best choice is a fabric sleeve, which will evenly distribute the weight of the quilt across the top edge, rather than at selected spots where tabs or rings are stitched, keep the quilt hanging straight and not damage the batting.

To make a sleeve, measure across the top of the finished quilt. Cut an 8"-wide piece of muslin equal to that length—you may need to seam several muslin strips together to make the required length.

Fold in 1/4" on each end of the muslin strip and press. Fold again and stitch to hold. Fold the muslin strip along length with right sides together. Sew along the long side to make a tube. Turn the tube right side out; press with seam at bottom or centered on the back.

Hand-stitch the tube along the top of the quilt and the bottom of the tube to the quilt back making sure the quilt lies flat. Stitches should not go through to the front of the quilt and don't need to be too close together as shown in Figure 32.

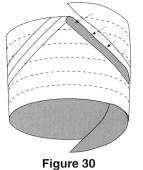

Figure 32
Sew a sleeve to the top back of the quilt.

Slip a wooden dowel or long curtain rod through the sleeve to hang.

When the quilt is finally complete, it should be signed and dated. Use a permanent pen on the back of the quilt. Other methods include cross-stitching your name and date on the front or back or making a permanent label which may be stitched to the back.

SPECIAL THANKS

We would like to thank the talented quilt collectors and designers whose work is featured in this collection.

Ann Boyce
Starry Nine-Patch Pillows, 46
Pig in a Nine-Patch, 99
Chambray Skirt & Vest, 145

Chris Carlson
Floral Bouquet, 33

Xenia E. Cord
Continuous Nine-Patch, 12
Cut Glass Dish, 23
Milky Way Crib Quilt, 113

Michele Crawford
Nine-Patch Bathroom Set, 49

Holly Daniels
Twist & Turn Nine-Patch, 93
Funky Fish Lap Quilt, 121

Lucy Fazely
Harbinger of Spring, 78
Miniature Nine-Patch, 83
Ribbon & Stars Quilt, 85

Goose in the Barn, 89
Seeing Spots, 107
Storm at Sea, 131

Sandra L. Hatch
Musical Chairs, 19
Eight-Pointed Star, 29
True Lover's Knot, 103
I Heard It Through
    the Grapevine, 109

Melody Johnson
Nouveau Nine-Patch, 118

Pauline Lehman
Antique Nine-Patch, 27

Joyce Livingston
Forever Spring, 95

Janice McKee
Nine-Patch Dresser Scarf &
    Treasure Box, 40
Contemporary Nine-Patch, 141

Connie Rand
Call of the Wild, 125

Sherry Reis
Seashore Stars, 55
Ladders by the Sea, 59

Carol Scherer
Rainbow of Rings, 15

Marian Shenk
Welcome Banner, 63

Beth Wheeler
Dolly & Me, 67
Bedroom Ensemble, 71
Nine-Patch Cardigan Sweatshirt, 128
Quilter's Tote, 135
Nine-Patch Purse, 138

Angie Wilhite
Birdhouse Place Setting, 43

PHOTO CREDITS

Special thanks to Limberlost State Historical Site, Geneva, Ind., and Swiss Heritage Village, Berne, Ind., for photography on location.

FABRICS & SUPPLIES

Page 33: Floral Bouquet—BiRangle ruler and Baby Bias Square from That Patchwork Place, Mettler Metrosene Polyester thread, Collins silk pins.

Page 43: Birdhouse Place Setting—Dual Duty Plus rayon embroidery and all-purpose threads, transparent nylon monofilament and bias tape from Coats & Clark, Wonder-Under fusible webbing, Sof-Shape interfacing, Quilter's Fleece and Stitch-n-Tear fabric stabilizer from Pellon.

Page 46: Starry Nine-Patch Pillows—Mission Valley Textiles fabrics.

Page 78: Harbinger of Spring—RJR Fashion Fabrics, Mountain Mist Quilt Light batting, Snap Shot ruler and templates from Sew/Fit Co.

Page 83: Miniature Nine-Patch—Mountain Mist Batting, SnapShot ruler from Sew/Fit.

Page 85: Ribbon & Stars Quilt—RJR Fashion Fabrics, Mountain Mist batting.

Page 89: Goose in the Barn—RJR Fashion Fabrics, Warm & Natural Cotton batting, ruler from Sew-Fit Co.

Page 107: Seeing Spots—Mountain Mist Light batting, ruler from Sew-Fit Co.

Page 109: I Heard It Through the Grapevine—Springs Industries Fabrics.

Page 118: Nouveau Nine-Patch—YLI Wonder thread, ARTFABRIK fabric from Melody Johnson and Laura Wasilowski.

Page 131: Storm at Sea—Warm & Natural Cotton batting, SnapShot ruler by Sew/Fit Co.

Page 145: Chambray Skirt and Vest—Mission Valley Textiles fabrics.